BECOME A *Rock Star*
REAL ESTATE AGENT

BECOME A
Rock Star
REAL ESTATE
AGENT

7 STEPS TO
MAKE $100K
A YEAR

JENNIFER SEENO TUCKER

NEW YORK

LONDON • NASHVILLE • MELBOURNE • VANCOUVER

BECOME A *Rock Star* REAL ESTATE AGENT
7 STEPS TO MAKE **$100K** A YEAR

© 2021 **JENNIFER SEENO TUCKER**

Published in New York, New York, by Morgan James Publishing in partnership with Difference Press. Morgan James is a trademark of Morgan James, LLC. www.MorganJamesPublishing.com

ISBN 978-1-63195-026-1 paperback
ISBN 978-1-63195-027-8 eBook
ISBN 978-1-63195-028-5 Audio
Library of Congress Control Number: 2020901833

Cover Design Concept:
Jennifer Stimson

Cover Design:
Rachel Lopez
www.r2cdesign.com

Editor:
Nkechi Obi

Book Coaching:
The Author Incubator

Morgan James is a proud partner of Habitat for Humanity Peninsula and Greater Williamsburg. Partners in building since 2006.

Get involved today! Visit
www.MorganJamesBuilds.com

For Jaden, my lovie, thank you for always reminding me to take the bumps in the road with laughter and a smile, just like the one in New Jersey after softball. You are forever my saving angel.

TABLE OF CONTENTS

Chapter 1

SPIN YOU AROUND, BLURRY—
PUDDLE OF MUDD

*Y*ou're never really ready for when your whole life changes. For me, that day was September 1, 2007. I was visiting family here in New York while my husband was in Wyoming, where we lived for a couple years. He was in a serious car accident—serious enough that I immediately flew back west after being in New York for only twelve hours. The nearest level trauma hospital that was able to care for his injuries was in

Montana. No one on the phone would tell me the severity of it, so when I approached his room in the ICU to find him on a ventilator with a shunt in his head, a broken back and hip, and in an induced coma, my mouth dropped to the floor. I nearly fainted and wept beyond belief. I had never cried like that— never felt an emotion so strong that I did that night. It was the saddest day of my life.

Our daughter was fifteen months old. I had left her in New York while I attended to her father. When I asked the doctors if he was going to make it, they said to me, "Let's see what happens in the next thirty days." Being the courageous, brave, stonewall person my dad had taught me to be in situations like this, I just shook my head and said "OK."

OK? Was I crazy? Who just replies back OK? That was the first time I had surrendered. Given up. I had to let go of control. I mean, what could I do? I had always fought back under almost any circumstance. My fist was constantly pounding my hand, but this time there was no punching. I wasn't in the driver's seat. The only people who could help him were the doctors. They were the professionals. I couldn't rescue him—save him from this trauma. Or could I?

I went to chapel every day and prayed. I asked God for help to guide my husband back to us, for he was only twenty-seven at the time. I hadn't been to church in nearly ten years except for our wedding day; I didn't know if I was being heard or not, but I figured it couldn't hurt.

He was in a coma for nine weeks before "waking up," which definitely doesn't look like it does on a daytime soap opera. It was a very slow process, and it little by little wore me down. My daughter was *still* staying in New York—a tough decision to make, but I couldn't take care of her, give her the love and support she required as a sixteen-month-old, as my time was consumed by tending to her dad. Dealing with doctors, insurance companies, and in-laws was a full-time job—an exhausting full-time job that required executive decisions to be made at a moment's notice. I was also staying in a hotel room long-term just to be close to the hospital. Financially, our little bit of savings that we did have was wiped out between lodging and food.

After he woke up from his coma, I no longer knew who I was. I had gained thirty pounds and began working for our town within the parks department scrubbing public toilet bowls for pool patrons. I had my master's degree, and I was scrubbing the remainder of someone's lunch off this can of filth. I needed this job. I had to take it, out of desperation, to stay close to home should my husband have an emotional breakdown and not tend to the needs of our daughter. This civil servant job was the only job I could work that would afford me the time to deal with my family's unfortunate situation. I was earning twelve dollars an hour, and although it was more than what the college kids were making, in New York supporting a family of three, it was difficult to survive. We utilized every federal, state, and local government program that was out there, including food stamps, WIC (Women Infant Children), Medicare, and the Daycare Assistance Program. The mere thought, let alone the days I had to enter the social security offices were agonizing and embarrassing. I hated it so much I can recall puking outside the office of my social worker. Of course, she asked if I was pregnant—I wasn't! Paying bills was nearly impossible. I was late with the minimum payment every month, there was no catching up, and I couldn't see the light at the end. I felt as if I was drowning and began getting a ringing in my ears from all the stress. Our car, which became an Uber not for hire, taxied my husband from doctor to doctor. It was on its last leg. And eventually, I filed for bankruptcy.

I was beyond humiliated and mortified to be in this position and retreated from family functions even further. I felt unworthy to be in their presence because I couldn't support my family. I've heard people grow and transform through either insight or suffering. There was definitely no meaningful evolution occurring here, so at this stage of my life, it was definitely the latter.

Over a seven-year period, my husband did make a miraculous recovery, but his chronic condition ultimately was the death of our marriage. Caring for him was a full-time job as I tended to his daily life skills and assisted him with getting washed, dressed and brushing his teeth. I was more of a nurse and caretaker than a wife. He was not the same person I married. As a result of his brain injury, he became violent and hot tempered and would make impulsive inappropriate spending decisions online, and his attitude about life was extremely negative. But this was our situation and I accepted it until one day I didn't. I was not willing to just "exist" for the sake of the relationship without having any purpose or meaning any longer. I had finally hit the limit where I wanted more for myself than I was getting.

On to the life of single parenting. I was still scrubbing toilets but felt I could be utilizing my background in physical education to open my own children's fitness business. I think I was motivated to make such a big bold move by watching *Shark Tank*. I always wanted to be my own boss, as I hated answering to people, but complied most of the time because that's what good girls do. Additionally, I admired my mother as an entrepreneur. I mean, she was super successful and had managed to put us through private school and college as a real estate agent. In her office one day, consulting with her about my lack of growth in my business, her secretary had given her a paper on a rental lead to follow up with. She literally took the lead, crumbled it up, and tossed it in the garbage.

I exclaimed, "*What* are you doing? That's a lead, which you could convert. Why did you throw it away?"

"I don't have time for rentals. I'm way too busy working with buyers and sellers," she said.

Well, I had the time, so I told myself, "OK, go get your real estate license."

I picked up the phone right then and there and enrolled in the course. I completed it in three months and became licensed in December 2012. I wasn't going to fail again and felt supported in my decision. It really felt right, which catapulted my quest for top producer in real estate. I was eager and hungry—I mean literally. My daughter and I began our game to find the best brand of macaroni and cheese out there.

I managed to start in real estate just working with the renters, which ran me ragged, and in New York, I was getting my workout climbing up and down stairs, but I appreciated the knowledge and learning curve in how to navigate through a transaction. It also allowed for opportunities to make mistakes without costing me too much. It was a natural learning curve.

Dealing with renters also gave me experience in talking and communicating what I was trying to say. I was always the "shy one," as Mom had always explained. It ultimately became me— who I identified with—and I took on the personality and made it my own. But in hindsight, I was always deep in thought, consistently observing people's behavior and analyzing their actions and reactions. It was observing in my early childhood that led me to be a very talented athlete. By analyzing people, I became calculated and could anticipate a change, a shift in the decision-making process of my opponent. I was so good at it that I earned a full athletic scholarship to college. The combination of my background in sports, basketball and softball, and as a physical education teacher as well as my ability to be agile and anticipate the reactions of others was the *perfect* combination for real estate sales.

The chaotic nature of real estate brought out the athlete in me, as I could pivot and turn, adjust and adapt, and think on the spot for any objection a prospect would shoot my way. *Swish*! It was a slam dunk every time.

But I was never home. My daughter was that latchkey kid. She learned how to make her own mac and cheese with some one-on-one FaceTime. And soon, it was scrambled eggs, and at one point, I think I walked her through baking chicken in the oven. She became the chef of the house.

We were lucky enough to have a roof over our heads for minimal rent—at Mom's house. So, I was working with mom, living with her in her house, and of course we would travel together to go see family. To say this didn't put a strain on the spiritual bonding of a mother-daughter relationship is being kind. She was consistently the parent at home and at work and I was consistently the child, a mere eight years old, whenever we had any business or family related conversation. Over that period, we must've broken up our business partnership at least twenty times. But our teamed-up business was really doing well.

That's right: I had moved up to putting chicken on the table.

We always said to prospects that I did the walking and she did the talking, which I didn't mind because I lost twenty pounds. But it wasn't the walking that helped me lose and keep off all those boxes of macaroni and cheese I had eaten. It was the feel good of making my own money, out-right owning my own car, and earning the trust of clients on my own. I was an entrepreneur. Making my own decisions and leading my business in the direction I wanted it to go.

I loved the freedom real estate allowed for me. I could come and go as I pleased, work or not work at my own pace, without having some administrator or supervisor at my back requesting my lesson plans and then critiquing them with his red pen and making me revise them to his standards. Most of my working years were spent as a physical education teacher in both the public and private school settings for ten years, and I developed empathy for my students. I truly enjoyed watching them grow, but I was never quite felt comfortable teaching, and raising other people's children was simply weird. Moreover, I liked to teach lessons my way, no matter what red ink was scribbled across my page. I hated that some admin would tell me what I needed in my classroom when he was there to observe for forty-five minutes one day in a180-day school year.

As an agent I was working hard all the time. There wasn't a day I missed, and I knew I was earning the respect of my father, for he believed that working *hard* will get you places. The harder you work, the further in life you will go. He worked his butt off, all the time. So much so that he never attended any of my athletic games or school events. I could see I was the same way as my father, working about ten- to twelve-hour days, seven days a week. It didn't matter when someone rang my phone, I was there to answer it, and I was there to show a house no matter what that interrupted in my life. It was completely random and chaotic, yet I also thrived in the chaos of real estate—the random people and interactions with others. No matter what time of day—late at night or early in the morning—there is always someone I could talk to about real estate. It literally took over my life. The videos I was watching, the coaches I was listening to, the seminars I was attending—I was spending a lot of money listening to other people talk about real estate. But I couldn't get enough of it. I wanted more, and I knew I was meant for more.

My personality likes the quick rewards, and the money I was making wasn't quick enough as I wanted it, which is why I dove headfirst even further. No matter what the circumstances were or who was hurt, or what family birthday party or anniversary wedding was missed, there was always a reason to put these family events aside. That reason was real estate and that I had to make money. I had to put food on the table. I had to support my daughter. Money was the main objective—it was my only means to survive. I mean, I had lived without money after my husband's accident, and that was difficult, it was hurtful, and it was so much pain and so much disgrace not being able to provide for my family. I withdrew from life—from the essence of my being.

During this time, my body ached on a consistent basis. Each night I would attend to my daughter and read books to her. I loved that time we would spend quietly together. But instead of a reading routine, I would fall asleep in my daughter's bed all the time and could barely make it through *A Fly Went By*. I constantly had a numbing in my ears, and I was seeing a chiropractor at least once a week.

My business stagnated over the next year or so, and I was making somewhere between $50,000 and $70,000 annually. It was good money, I didn't have too many bills, and I was able to put some chicken on the table. But I wanted more. I wanted to be successful, and I didn't feel successful with me earning this much money. I was still working part time scrubbing toilet bowls for some extra cash as well. I knew if I could transition to a full-time agent, I could really earn $100,000, even the possibility of more, but I didn't know how to do it. I didn't have the means or the skills or the time. I definitely had the desire, but it wasn't happening. I could see what other agents were doing, but I didn't have the past clients like they had. I didn't have the ability to speak to people in a meaningful way like they did. Their experience brought them to where they were, and I was only in the business for a short period time.

I kept thinking, *If I could just earn more money, my problems would be solved.* I would be able to put steak on the table as opposed to chicken. I could see my chiropractor twice a week as opposed to just once. My relationships would be cohesive, and I would be able to move out of my mother's house. So, I could see the problem, but I didn't know how to fix it. I didn't know what I needed. I didn't know what to do. I was pretty down on myself and depressed. The sadness was overwhelming for me, and I didn't see it coming. But my daughter did.

"Mommy what's wrong with you? Is everything OK? You look so sad."

I couldn't hear her. She knew more than I did how much pain I was in.

Chapter 2

FOLLOW YOU DOWN—
SHINEDOWN

When I first went into real estate, I thought this would be an easy endeavor.

Make calls, show properties, and get paid.

That's it.

I thought I could do this with my eyes closed. I have a Master of Science degree for goodness sake.

I was hired as a buyer's agent, an apprentice if you will, but at times the job was more like a gopher. I would run here and there opening doors for buyers and other agents who were showing the lead agent's listings. Other times, I was collecting contracts all over the county. I was even playing administrator, setting up, confirming, and even canceling appointments for the lead agent. I was happy to be a part of a team, and I did enjoy learning from the ground up. Without this platform to gain experience from, I would have been a one hit wonder like Harvey Danger. Go YouTube their song "Flagpole Sitta"—then you'll know what I'm talking about. Yet having these multiple roles has set the tone and my expectations for what my business is today. Gradually, more responsibility was given to me, and I would come into the office and help out experienced, frustrated agents with their first-time home buyers, guiding them to finding their dream home with some updated technology and a fresh set of legs. I imagined this would be a simple process since these agents couldn't be bothered working with first-time home buyers as they seemed easily frustrated by working with them.

I became a real estate agent in December 2012. I figured I would be giving an overview of the buying process so that buyers, specifically first-time buyers, would avoid some costly mistakes; in addition, I would also help the buyers determine the size, style, and benefits of the home that would be a good fit for their families' needs. I could make my own schedule, and buyers would work around me and my time. This would grow my business and fill my pockets in no time.

Yeah, I was wrong.

I had no clear path about where to find the best buyers or sellers to be working with or what they looked like. I thought I should be working with every single person who called me or walked into the office no matter where they were in their buying or selling stage, so I was answering my phone at all hours of the day because I never knew who was calling me to work with them. After some time of this, I began to feel used and abused, unwanted and unworthy. These buyers and sellers were like kids in a candy store, scanning the aisle, carefully searching for the right piece of chocolate to satisfy their craving. In essence, the prospect was gathering all the information they needed to make an informed decision about me as a real estate agent, but I was the one spilling my candy in the lobby. I was giving them all the facts, figures, and particulars about what kind of agent I was. To top it all off, they never notified me that they weren't going to hire me either. Kind of rude.

But they were not the ones to blame. It was me who was giving them permission to gather all the information they needed to purchase or sell a home through someone else because I was trying to please them and answer all of their questions even when I didn't know the answer. It was me who wanted to meet all of their needs in their time. This made it difficult for the prospect to decide if I was a good fit for them to be working with.

I can recall sitting in a home located in a suburban neighborhood and being interviewed by a seller, a prospect who had reached out to me from my "Premier Agent" status on a certain website. This was a four-bedroom, two-and-half-bath colonial between $500k and $550k.

I was stopped mid-spiel by the customer's words. Wait, what? Did you say $500k to $550k, (the average home sales price at the time was approximately $350K in this neighborhood). My fantasies of top producer were "jamming out" in my head as a foreseeable thought into the future. It was like Nirvana playing "Smells Like Teen Spirit."

Yes, I thought, this would be my payday. I was sitting in a 2,400-square-foot newly constructed colonial home with four queen-sized bedrooms and two and half baths and featuring front-to-rearview sightline, custom cherry wood cabinetry, hardwood oak flooring throughout, and a gorgeous granite-topped kitchen with a Tuscan tile backsplash, as well as ample closet space and a fully finished basement for family entertainment. My potential commission of $28K was nearly one-third away from my income goal. Hear that—it's Lucy playing in the sky with diamonds.

The standard questions from the seller were asked. How much can I get for my home? How's the market? Is now the right time to sell?

After asking all their pressing questions, the prospects said, "Thank you, Jennifer. My wife and I are going to think it over and let you know."

To which I replied, "Perfect, Mr. Seller! Looking forward to your call."

After leaving the home, I majestically walked to my car. The presentation went well, and I left there feeling really good that they were probably going to hire me as their agent.

I sent a thank-you card the next day, followed up with a text the day after, and even dropped a spring flower box at their door. Everything all the big trainers from YouTube videos and local seminars had instructed me to do. After a week of this, there was still no listing agreement. They must be busy, I thought. But the homeowner did not leave a voicemail in my new, upgraded, fancy, *free* app, YouMail, either. Hmmmmm, what was happening?

On Monday of the next week, I saw the home come out on the MLS, and I wasn't the listing agent. I was crushed. I felt sick to my stomach. My mouth was watering. I drove home. I didn't know why I felt this way. I was unsure how I was feeling and what was going on. This didn't make any sense. Then I threw up in my mouth.

I think I was down to about $100 in my bank account, my credit card payment was past due, and there was only a quarter of a tank of gas left in my car.

What was I missing? Why wasn't I hired? I did the presentation the exact way I was instructed to give it.

Then it hit me! In writing lesson plans as a teacher, I would have to always know what outcome I wanted to achieve by the end of the forty-five-minute lesson. This set a clear expectation for my role and what I was going to cover during the class. It also allowed my students to know where we were going and how we were going to get there –absolutely no surprises. Everything was outlined *prior* to the bell ringing of class.

I was giving my seller and buyer client presentations without an agenda. There was no mutual agreement or upfront contract (UFC) about what was going to happen at the end of the presentation. I needed to have an agreement in place with the prospect *before* we even met. I needed to be able to communicate with the prospect what outcome was going to occur by the end of the sales presentation. I was either going to be hired or not.

Surprises at birthday parties are so much fun. There's laughter everywhere. But in business, they are deal breakers. By presenting the prospect with an upfront verbal contract, we could remove any mystery from the presentation. It's also important for the real estate salesperson to be in control of the sales process and eliminate any unexpected elements. It is a tool that helps bring clarity to both the prospect and the agent herself.

In the ninety days after altering my presentation and setting the outcomes of my presentation on the phone call prior to meeting the prospect, I had four listings and five buyer clients, and my pipeline was filled with future business.

What was the difference from the previous years I had been busting my butt running around aimlessly?

It was a definite outcome and result in a precise time frame, with a specific agent. *Me*!

This isn't rocket science. And you don't have to spend lots of marketing dollars or time making it work. Heck, you already have a phone and an email account. That's all you need. You don't need social media, you don't need to be part of a team, you don't need click funnels, you don't need videos. You need you to be present and show up.

And your presentation doesn't have to be a perfect masterpiece in order for it make sense to your prospects. Because while you are still perfecting your presentation, you can offer your prospects a discounted commission and lots of personalized time as they may be your only client. Your value proposition increases. So, you win, and the prospect most certainly wins too.

Don't get me wrong, failure is going to happen. Not every prospect is going to be a good fit for your real estate business.

But I would rather you fail by going for a no rather than a "think it over." Having a super clear and concise future is the name of the real estate game. So, stop thinking you're not going to be able to service the client properly, feeling overwhelmed by the vast amount of knowledge you need to be a top-producing agent, and putting pressure, real elephant-standing-on-your-chest pressure, on yourself to get the signature. You're self-sabotaging, and you will never be able to let go of that paycheck from your job, close more deals, and become a top-producing real estate agent if you are not willing to invest in yourself and experience moments that are uncomfortable that will lead to change.

I promise, if are saying to your co-agents, broker, and family members that you are frustrated and confused, worried and upset, anxious and concerned, you're not going to earn enough money in real estate to stick it out, and then you are *choosing* to stay comfortable making the monies in your real estate business you are making right now.

Don't get me wrong, I lost more listing presentations after that, but what changed with that was I wasn't afraid to fail. Getting the signature on the contract page didn't make me who I was, but it did shape me to be better equipped with rejection and a more effective real estate agent

So, stop *deciding* that you're not good at selling real estate or you're not cut out for this business, and start accepting that you're going to have to make hard choices to make a $100k in your real estate business.

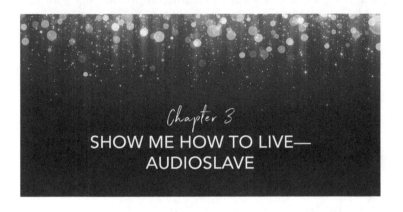

Chapter 3

SHOW ME HOW TO LIVE— AUDIOSLAVE

*F*or many real estate agents, making $100k can be tough. First, you must do the hard work of going back to school to get a real estate license and certification. Then, you have to be consistent with your marketing and sales process and, after that, crush the industry by closing deals on a weekly basis, which can take several years. It can be extremely intense and overwhelming if you're holding down another job too.

So, let's talk.

I've been in the business for eight years but have been listening to advice about the field for thirty years, as my mother is also a broker. But what I've learned from working with real estate agents on increasing production is that it's important to utilize the skills you already have and transfer them into the real estate business. They are your biggest assets, and your clients will appreciate you more for your honesty in the process. It sets the stage as a foundation for the type of real estate career you will have and the type of real estate business you will run to set you up for the future.

I also think choosing the right brokerage and selecting the right coaches and mentors are so important to your real estate career. They lay the building blocks in your training, branding, and the culture and ethics you bring into the real estate business. So, if earning $100k or more is the outcome you want to achieve, don't take this part of your decision-making process lightly. Do your research prior to completing your certification. And if you want to earn $100k or more in this business by helping and assisting property owners buy and sell real estate, make a difference in their lives so that you become their real estate agent for life and the one they are referring all their friends and family to—you don't want to leap over the amplifier because on the other side you'll be smashing your guitar and maybe your head in the process.

If you don't know too much about selecting the right brokerage, you're not alone and you're bound to get confused at one point or another. Let me tell you, it's not about the commission splits or where your friends or family have placed their licenses but about the training and culture that your office will give you as a newer agent. Additionally, find the brokerage that is located in and has market share in your niche market, whether that's residential, luxury or condo sales, or even investment properties. Find the brokerage that suits your passion. After all, your goal is to be a rock star, to be the most popular real estate agent in the neighborhood, and you will need your "business family" to give you the support, encouragement, and training necessary to reach your goal.

Most new real estate agents don't know how buyers and sellers select them to be their agent, so it's OK to settle for the scraps your broker throws at you. These aren't going to be the A leads who are buying and selling real estate today. They are the B's and C's who are looking to buy and sell three to twelve months from now. Work them as if they are As because you are putting in effort and creating daily success habits. Use these leads to practice your script skills and refine your sales pitch. I recommend using a weekly email to stay in touch with these prospects to keep yourself in front of them.

And finally, get in the office. You will learn the most by just being present and listening to experienced agents talk the real estate lingo and negotiate. Volunteer to host an open house, a home inspection, or even closings, just because you want to learn. Hand deliver contracts to meet attorneys, run a market analysis report of your friends' and family members' homes. Anything you can do to boost your real estate knowledge in the shortest amount of time—do it!

My goal for you through this real estate journey in this book is to help you identify the avenues to keep your business growing on a deliberate path of prosperity and wealth. To begin creating the favorable circumstances that will increase your likelihood for success and an effective, long-lasting, full-time real estate sales career.

Yet it is of utter importance that you understand the steps to becoming a Rock star real estate agent took years of practice, refinement, and failure. Becoming Barbara Corcoran will not magically happen. The best part of this is that it's all your choice, your decision to take what knowledge you want out of this book and apply it to your real estate career. You'll find certain topics may correlate to what's currently occurring in your real estate business, and they will resonate like light bulb moments for you to scribble notes for reference.

As your confidante, I assure you are a Rock star real estate agent right now, and you don't even know it! So if you are interested in a fast track to acquiring your next listing, closing your next deal, and living a financially freeing life, this book is your gateway to receiving the applause, praise, and groupies—yes, groupies—you've desired.

My broker soon realized I was making awesome progress and getting results for both my real estate business as well as hers, and I was hired to begin training new agents as they were sponsored into the company in the Seven Saturdays Training program I co-created. The goal here was to provide new agents entering the real estate field with a stepping-stone to grasp the activities and daily success habits, which we will explore in further detail in a later chapter, of real estate as a career and allow them to see that it is possible to transition from part-time agent to full time in a matter of months. I always tell my agents that if you want to break the monetary ceiling you've been settling for, it's time to focus on the difference you want to make in the industry. This precision will result in seeing more results in their real estate business.

So, what are the seven steps to achieving the real estate career you desire and Rock star real estate agent status?

1. **Premise and Purpose Strategy**: Having a pre-set notion of goals means we begin at the end first. You start with having authentic outcomes for your real estate career so there is a vision of your life.

2. **Establish a Farm Area**: It will take a prospect nine times to remember you, and they can't buy from you

if they don't know who you are, so getting in front of your audience increases your chances for success.

3. **Define Your Client**: It's essential to get clear on who the best prospects to be working with throughout your real estate career are, to know the difference between a customer and a client, and how to leverage your market.

4. **Having Systems in Place**: In order to guarantee you will have a prosperous real estate career, it is essential we go from knowing to owning the best practices, which will allow for real estate growth.

5. **Imagining Success**: The creation of a mental picture of your road map to success allows you to get a clear idea of the real estate career you were meant to have. Becoming honest with yourself about your needs, wants, and desires will allow for the abundant life you always envisioned.

6. **Removing Obstacles from Growth**: The number-one mistake new real estate agents make is starting from a place of force and "making things happen." Exploring and understanding how to align your mind, body, and spirit and the actions needed to overcome the bumps in the road are key concepts needed to overcome periods of stillness and stagnation in your business.

7. **Focusing on Relationships over Transactions**: There will always be greedy people in the world—it's human

nature—so if we take money out of the equation, what do you have? You want to get super clear that you are in the service business of meeting the needs of your clients.

These steps are easy to utilize and put into your everyday real estate routines. It's a formula that all top producers use to reach the next level in their real estate goals. The process is a catalyst to become a leading entrepreneur with assured monetary gains to start earning $100k while living a financially freeing lifestyle.

So if people have been telling you you're great for real estate, that they are so happy you are their real estate agent, or that you should do this full time, then you've come to the right place to release your fears and inhibitions. Let go of unwanted feelings of control, and you don't have to wait for the other parts of your life to fall into place. Your real estate community needs you to be their Rock Star Real Estate Agent!

Chapter 4

OPEN MY EYES— BUCKCHERRY

There's this perceived notion that becoming a real estate agent is easy. That it's a matter of taking a course, passing a test, getting some business cards and then—*poof*—money is rolling in. You go on to list a few houses, work with a few buyers, and you're crushing the business, which means everyone can do it. But there's a lot of competition out there. Just having your license does not make you a Rock star real estate agent, nor does it make you any money.

But these are all misconceptions because, as we all know, life gets in the way. You're dealing with kids, managing your home, and you may also be working another job because it's nearly impossible to quit your full-time job. After all, how are you going to pay the bills?

And that's exactly how my thinking began in real estate as well.

So, there came a point where I had to ask myself, "What am I going to do differently to set myself apart from the ten agents in the office or from the twenty thousand others in my county? How do I manage to create a real estate career on my own terms?"

Now, many people told me that in order to be a Rock star real estate agent, I first had to give up everything. So, there was no watching movies with my daughter, forget being able to scoot off on a cruise to Bermuda or even enjoy a glass of Chardonnay at my girlfriend's birthday party. To be ultra-successful in your new real estate career, in any new career, Napoleon Hill says, "you must have a 'white hot obsession' with it, so you must remove all those luxuries in your life in order to be successful." Is he speaking about *all* my time? Ummm, where's the fun in this business if that's what I'm doing and not doing for the next twelve months? After all, I went into a real estate career to make money, not to lose my life in the process. So, you'll be constantly grinding as hard as you possibly can, day in and out, losing sleep. I wasn't convinced this was the way to go. As a single mother, I barely had any time for me as it was, so there had to be another way.

And there was.

I began to think of my teaching background and how for ten years I had to create a curriculum for my students. This kind of sends me back a little bit further—during a summer class back in 2001 at Queens College doing my master's degree. We had to design an entire year's curriculum focused on a long-term objective, an outcome that you want the students to achieve by the end of the year. For example, by the end of the school year, students will gain an understanding that by proficiently performing moderate to vigorous physical activity in combination with strategic planning and tactical knowledge, they will improve their performance of various motor skills over a lifetime. This was followed by a short-term goal, which is the daily goal of the day. For example, students will be able to dribble a soccer ball through cones successfully five out of seven times.

In many ways, real estate is the same. We must first focus on our short-term goal in order to meet the long-term objective. Therefore, I began to ask myself, what is it that I want to achieve in real estate, and what are my long-term plans in real estate? Why did I go into this business? These are really the first questions to ask in figuring out a plan of action to take to become the most successful person you want to be in this business. After all, it is the way that you are going to provide food on the table for your family. Initially, in real estate, it was a matter of putting macaroni and cheese on the table every night for my daughter as I went through the ups and downs of the business. At times, I would walk into my office, sit there for an hour, and wait. But what was I waiting for?

Initially, I was being too passive, waiting for business to come to me when I was the one who needed to be active and take control of the business I was going to lead. I was afraid of the rejection. I was constantly hearing the no's and being hurt beyond belief, as if my parents were saying, "No you can't have that new bike." I took things way too personally, was insulted, and felt super rejected and abandoned.

Another inhibition that arose was the fear of talking about money and, even worse, other people's money. As I would sit with a buyer and ask, "How much of your savings do you have for a down payment," I could feel my body tighten up and my face crinkle as I asked the question. I soon learned my money blocks were from a childhood of listening to my parents fight and argue about savings, spending, and bills. Then there was the lag and lull in between commission checks. This real estate roller coaster ride of profit coming in seemed like the Aerosmith ride, Rock 'n' Roller Coaster at Disney World—*0 to 60 miles per hour in 2.8 seconds*. An initial blastoff filled with turns and pivots, ups and downs, sent my head spinning in all directions, lasting only seventy-five seconds. It left me thinking, "That's it?"

Yet as you exit the ride, there's your smiling face on camera because you loved all seventy-five seconds of it. That's real estate at its core.

So, what is it that you want to achieve? What is it that you want to have as a result in this crazy chaotic real estate world? What long-term goals do you want as a real estate agent? Making money is never the answer; it's just a byproduct of servicing your clients and meeting them where they are. The money will follow once you get in check with who you are and what struggles and challenges you are facing.

I'm sure you're thinking that this test is too massive or too unnerving; however, I came to approach this test without hesitation and fear. I realized that no two people would do this exactly the same; there's no single right way to go about it. We are all born different. It's a matter of taking a fearless moral inventory of yourself and writing down your strengths and weaknesses in black and white as an honest and completely objective aid.

Now, as you read through your list, it may be uncomfortable. I mean so uncomfortable that you may feel nauseous and want to puke, but if you can think of this process as something like peeling an onion, you can really only do it one layer at a time, and there's often going to be many bitter tears as you cut through each layer and look deeper into yourself. The good news is the very qualities that helped you support your family and raise your earnings at your salaried job are the same qualities you need to use in real estate.

It's the persistent and consistent behaviors that will drive you to be a true, authentic Rock star real estate agent. University of Virginia psychologist Jonathan Haidt says in order to adhere to a consistent and persistent mind-set, we should notice thoughts about stopping a task and make a conscious effort to dismiss them. So, if your goal is to make $100k as a real estate agent, which I hope it is since you are reading this book, focus on the task at hand, find a system that works and actually use it to set a goal and create a plan for sticking to it.

As I began to have some success in real estate, money was coming in, and I was taking care of my clients and listening to their needs, I was content but not living a fulfilled and happy life. I kept thinking, if there is food on the table, everything's gonna be OK. I don't have to be satisfied. But I was very unhappy in most of my outside work relationships, including the one with my daughter. I had begun to put on weight, was consistently sick with a cold, and my physical and mental state was in complete chaos. My mind was all over the place. It was so hard to focus on any one task at a time, and I had simply lost control of who I was.

My plan for creating a better vision of being a Rock star real estate agent began with having a Lifebook. I was introduced to John and Missy Butcher during a random 3:00 a.m. awakening, after taking two melatonin supplements to help me sleep. I opened my phone to play some YouTube videos and an ad for their Lifebook Mastermind class popped up and ran across my iPhone on this melatonin-induced night. They are like billionaires living this dream life from the fortunes they made in multiple companies, including Precious Moments. You know, those little figurines that you put on your mantel and buy in Hallmark stores? As I'm watching, I'm thinking, these are crazy people who just live in la la land, but for some reason, I continued to watch. They went on to outline important categories to focus on to have an extraordinary life. As I watched more and more, I couldn't help but think, how could I be complete and whole in happiness? Wasn't life meant to be lived in random chaos without any sense of direction? Isn't that how it was always done?

Then, *click*. The lights of the stage illuminated. It just made sense. I realize that my life's purpose was to authentically connect with others, have deeper, meaningful relationships on a soulful level, and to belong to a tribe while gaining financial freedom. That's simply what I wanted. And that's when I began to play my guitar solo at Madison Square Garden.

I went on to pay the $500 for their class and watch each of their hour-long coaching videos. At times, it was exhausting, but I developed the consistency, persistence, and discipline needed, which helped me outline twelve areas of my life where I could have a strategy and a pre-set notion of authentic goals all my own and not given to me by society. Each of the life categories—health and fitness, intellectual life, emotional life, character, spiritual life, love and relationship, parenting, social life, career, financial life, quality of life, and lastly life vision—allowed me to go deep within myself. I was able to authentically find my premise and purpose in each of the categories and then develop my own strategy for implementing the achievements and outcomes. What I learned was that I knew I had goals, but they were all in my head, scrambled and not clearly defined. I am not happy unless there is a goal for every aspect of my life, and I always need to be moving forward examining and probing toward a higher purpose. By having the Lifebook, I could physically reference my goals on a daily basis. I was able to consistently recall my life goals and know exactly how to apply my vision into my daily practices and focus on my purpose within the tasks. In essence I was in control of my life, which now had direction and purpose as opposed to just me floating and skimming the surface. This was a concrete vision of how I wanted to live my life. I didn't have to remember what my parenting goals were. I always had so many other things going on in my brain I couldn't immediately pull them out when I was having a difficult day with my daughter, but I could pull my Lifebook out and instantly revisit our amazing vacation in Costa Rica and how my goal was to be kinder and gentler with her feelings because that's where I had to meet her. My Lifebook allowed me to have my own personal intrinsic goals that I wanted. This video journey gave me a way to visualize and map out an ideal future. I was able to craft out a magnificent vision for myself and my family.

As I went on crafting out my life vision, I worked from the outside in. Focusing first on my personal life, including health and fitness. Next was the relationships category, including my relationship with money, and finally my overall life vision and quality of life. The Lifebook guided me toward having a singular compelling life vision one filled with happiness and success and crafting the ideal life I have always wanted. Don't get me wrong, I'm still on that journey, but it has definitely set me on the right path to being the person I want to become, intrinsically and extrinsically. Because of it, I am able to become the real Rock star real estate agent I want to be in my own business.

Having a Lifebook has helped me make amends in all my relationships and focus on the relationships that are truly important to me and that I am meant to have with my clients by just opening my ears more. I'm better at listening to the needs of my clients, and because of it I am a better parent.

I have found compassion for myself and developed a new awareness of my responsibility to my clients where previously I had embodied a philosophy of getting the deal done to get paid. It's a poor mind-set filled with the mentality of "what's in it for me?" This doesn't come from a place of compassion, nor does it service the client the way that should he or she should be serviced.

The Rock star real estate agents aren't born, they work at consistently fine-tuning the end result they want out of a career in real estate, persistently leverage themselves against the rest of the pack, stay ahead of the market, and service their clients. You can truly begin to deeply unleash the past and free yourself from the pressures of society to allow for the seeds of growth in real estate to take root for a financially freeing career once you make the commitment to feel good about you.

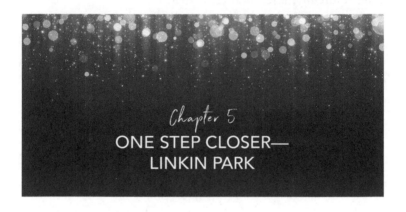

Chapter 5

ONE STEP CLOSER— LINKIN PARK

I grew up in a suburb of Manhattan about forty-five minutes away from downtown. A middle-class, blue-collar neighborhood. And then I went to the Catholic grammar school and high school, where I played basketball and softball in the community and church leagues. There was really nothing special about it, although it's pretty famous for the Belmont Stakes, which happen every year in June. It's one of the races in the Triple Crown. I tried to escape this neighborhood every chance I could get. I think I moved out of the house I grew up in approximately seven or eight times. Gosh, I can't even count anymore. It's been so many.

Now my dad's side had a small family-owned oil delivery business in the neighborhood, so there was a little bit of a celebrity status that I had growing up. My mother, a thirty-year veteran and top-producing agent in the real estate business herself, took advantage of this star-like situation and began marketing to the community as a real estate agent. She was always shaking hands, kissing babies, and helping older ladies cross the street.

I had moved back into the community after my husband's accident and became reacclimated with it. I grew up working part-time in the town park. I had been living out of state for almost four years. My daughter joined all the park activities, and I would see familiar faces on a consistent basis. I wanted to belong to something greater than me and was encouraged to join a community action group. So, I guess you can say that I didn't choose the market that I serviced as a real estate agent, it ultimately chose me.

It made no sense when I got my real estate license to go to a different neighborhood. I had to stay. I had to be the next generation of business owners who lived, worked, and played in the community.

What I'm trying to say here is that if you're serious about becoming the neighborhood real estate expert in your market area, you need to be personally invested in it and start acting like the unofficial town supervisor, be the code enforcer with complete comprehension of code compliance, understand rules and regulations as a new construction builder and investor, and have FEMA flood insurance knowledge. After all, the best politicians mix it up with community leaders, mingle with constituents (homeowners), show up to a variety of school functions, and, yes, they kiss babies and shake hands too.

Networking and Building Your Brand

Networking helped me come out of my introverted self. As a New York City physical education teacher, I typically taught lessons to fifty to sixty students at a time, which forced me to take on a different persona. Yet, to speak to professionals one-on-one, who I had just met, and tell them I was the hardest-working real estate agent in the county was nerve rattling and sent chills down my back like I had just jumped into a cold pool. *Brrr.* The drastic difference in these two scenarios came from a controlling aspect. My ego was definitely inflated as the leader of a classroom. There was a sense of power and authority knowing I was the one these teenagers were listening to. But I must say, as the fierce leader, I had a lot to learn. The harsh, drastic choice to blow a whistle to get students attention is a bad one. It doesn't get them to stop, look, and listen to you as the teacher and leader. It only disrespects their intelligence. As a result, during my one-on-one introductions with my peers, I felt inferior and like I didn't belong. Who was I for these powerful leaders in finance, law, and insurance to believe in me? The trick here was I actually didn't believe in myself as a leader, whether that was in front of the classroom or in real estate.

My fears would get the best of me. I knew I had to differentiate myself from my mother and create my own real estate brand as I knew one day I would be on my own. If I wanted to be a successful real estate agent and build my mission of earning $100k, I needed to surround myself with professionals who were more successful than I was. They became my accountability partners, and I deserved to be in the room with each of those affluent professionals Somehow, being my mother's minion made me feel limited and stunted. I mean, Mom did get me started in the business, but I wasn't going to be her administrator forever. It's the reason—or my *why* which we will talk about in a later chapter—I went into real estate.

My Sandler Institute sales coach, which I'll talk more about later, suggested I look into a networking group. Most of the ones I found online had already had a real estate agent in the group, but I managed to find one only twenty minutes away that had an opening. The group was about filled with around ten professionals, including several attorneys, a mortgage banker, a financial advisor, and an accountant. They congregated on Wednesday mornings at a local diner. So, I forced myself every Wednesday morning at 7:15 a.m. to go to a diner and give my thirty-second commercial on a live platform in front of ten successful professionals over an egg sandwich. It went something like this:

"Hi, I am Jennifer Seeno Tucker. I am a licensed real estate agent with Exit Realty United located in Nassau County, New York. For the past four years, I have been servicing buyers and sellers alike throughout Long Island and Queens. I typically work with homeowners throughout the counties who are:

- Concerned with the current changes in their neighborhood
- Feeling frustrated over the rising rate of taxes
- Feeling anxious about the current market value of their home
- Or are simply ready to move on to the next phase of their lives

Additionally, I enjoy working with investors and builders alike to fine-tune their marketing plans for new construction and remodeled homes. My passion is to work with first-time home buyers as it allows me to utilize my educational background to guide them through the transaction in finding their dream home."

Whew! I got through it.

This move helped me strengthen my real estate business and my brand. I knew I had to leverage my time for money initially. This was the way to go if homeowners were going trust me to list their homes. After all, homeowners are the best source of clients because:

1. They own homes
2. They know what they want when they are buying a home
3. They most likely have a network of people they know who own homes as well

So that's who my target audience was. Homeowners!

And it really doesn't matter if it's a BNI; an REIA; a PTA; the local Rotary, Kawana's, or political club; your chamber of commerce; a young professionals networking group; or even LeTip—join it and keep talking real estate.

Building Your Marketing Savvy

I soon realized, as I should've known before, I had no business and marketing experience whatsoever. How was I to get my name out in the neighborhood and the public and into my marketing community without any marketing plan or zero marketing monies? What was I to do? How was the public going to buy or list their home with me if they didn't know who I was? I didn't want to be a "secret agent." So, I began to circle prospects and farm an area around five hundred homes. Just to clarify, "circle prospecting" is when you pick an area within your market to specifically target; this could be a subdivision, a zip code, or just a smaller neighborhood within a community. I chose an area to farm based on price, location, and turnover rate. Here is how you can use the same criteria to narrow down an area of focus:

- **Price**: Choose a neighborhood and community within your market that have homes that are the median sales price.
- **Location**: Market knowledge will give you an advantage over other real estate agents working the same neighborhood. Be cognizant that 123 Everclear Way is owned by Art Alexakis now who bought it from the Smythe's eight years ago. And that Taylor's sister

lives at 321 Shotgun Lane with her husband, Fred. Immerse yourself in the community. Live, work, and play there, which we have already visited in Chapter 2 and earlier in this chapter.

- **Turnover Rate:** Focus on volume not the price point. The average first-time homeowner will stay in his home five to eight years before he needs to upgrade due to an expanding family, job relocation, or divorce. Yep, it's a fact! You will be able to complete more transactions in markets that are consistently turning over at a faster rate than other higher-end neighborhoods.

Once you've narrowed down your area of focus, then you have to determine your plan of attack.

The very first doors I knocked on, or white knuckled, were during the rain and snow. I like dressing professionally, probably because Mom always said, "dress for success." In my real estate business, I think it kind of sets me apart from the rest of the crowd, which is typically very casual, but when I began circle prospecting and knocking on doors, I knew I had to keep a pair of sneakers in the trunk at all times. Yet this was short-lived. I felt like I was wasting time, got bored with no one ever answering their doorbell, and had to consistently buy new sneakers every few months because my feet hurt. I was extremely lonely doing this.

I can remember one day preparing to knock on doors again by myself and realizing I was surrounded by people who had been in the business for over twenty years that worked in my office. There was nothing new, nothing sexy, nothing exciting about real estate that got them totally engulfed in the community we all worked in. I soon realized I was surrounded by old real estate marketing methods; their listings all had a sign with their name and picture on it, they took out an ad in the local paper, they had balloons at their open houses, and still used sign-in sheets. In order to differentiate myself, I took to the future and technology.

I saw that I could leverage my time better by making phone calls and circle prospecting at the subdivision I had been sending my postcards to for the last year. I could begin to establish relationships with those homeowners, gain their trust, and put them into my database. For every ten to fifteen blocks in the zip code I market in, there is a different feeling, culture, and climate, and I chose the one that best suited my knowledge and my relationships.

Next, I ramped up my social media presence. Like I said, I'm an introvert and don't typically like to be out there exposed to the "devils" of social media, so I chose only three avenues to focus on: Facebook, Instagram, and YouTube. My philosophy has always been videos over pictures as science has proven that people remember and retain more information if the material is in a video. Here is the breakdown of how each of these platforms can be used:

- **Facebook**: This is a really good platform to get your message out and speak to people from the heart. This social media avenue was most successful for me. Simply replying and *liking* the content of friends and family as well as in Facebook community groups has been most fruitful. I can say I have yielded approximately thirty transactions from this platform.
- **Instagram**: This is incredible for posting vibrant pics and walk-through videos of homes.
- **YouTube**: Creating a YouTube channel allowed me to reach and stay connected with a younger audience.

Finally, I started giving back to the community by donating school supplies at back-to-school nights, donating a portion of my commission to local charities, and hosting events. For example, I hosted a buyer seminar in the spring with my team of real estate experts who were part of my "dirty dozen," or the twelve people who are my preferred vendors. My team included an attorney, a loan officer, and a home inspector, and the events included a pumpkin pie giveaway at Thanksgiving and summer ice cream socials.

These relatively inexpensive events really got my name out to the community, branding me, and gave way to new insight into myself who I was as a real estate agent. I learned what I was capable of. I never knew that I could be this person who provided value to others and was gifted enough to assist buyers and sellers who sought me out. It was a realization that I was worthy of providing a service they couldn't achieve on their own. For example, buying a home of their dreams or selling an estate home. And once I slip into my high heels and my dress and drive to work, I become Jennifer the real estate agent –someone totally different than Jennifer the mother, sister, daughter, and friend.

But it was my own fear of failure that ultimately got in my own way.

Establishing Your Sales Strategy

I soon learned that I couldn't establish more business unless I had a BAT. And no I don't mean a baseball bat for smashing your competition or going after all the no's you heard in the past. I mean the behavior, attitude, and technique in acquiring a great sales process.

The BAT technique is a Sandler Sales training idea I learned while attend a coaching seminar. Below I've broken down each part of the technique:

- **Behavior** relates to having a structured method to the moneymaking activity. In essence, a step-by-step plan for reaching goals. Disorganized behavior will not bring you closer to success, nor will guesswork.

- **Attitude** has to do with your conscious awareness you have about yourself, your company, your service, and your marketplace. It can be one of possibility, or one of limitation. And since it's your perception, it's your choice.

- **Technique** relates to your skill set and your method of delivery. It consists of strategies and tactics you use for a particular purpose to elicit the particular behaviors of your prospects.

What I learned was whether it was my real estate sales career or my personal life, I could only achieve success as a result of these interrelated strategies. I couldn't ensure myself more business unless I had a plan, a belief, and an aligned work ethic that would work for me.

As I began to achieve more success in real estate, I realized that what I think and feel about the selling process and how I behaved during the selling process would greatly affect the outcome and success or failure of it. My prior beliefs, judgments, and actions that didn't support my goals sabotaged my own personal sales efforts. Therefore, an attitude and/or behavior adjustment, coupled with proven techniques, can be just the ticket to skyrocketing your outcomes.

So, who do you work with? Who are your raving fans? Before you define your ideal client, you must first get a clear understanding on who the best possible prospect is to be working with. Now not everyone is going to be a good fit, but you must find out who is and make a list of these people.

It can be nearly impossible to keep track of the number of prospects that you're going to meet without having a database or some sort of tracking system for your potential clients. Some years ago, I went snowmobiling through Yellowstone National Park. We rode ninety-six miles through the beautiful Rocky Mountains. It was such a freeing experience and provided me with a great connection to nature and the wonders within her peaks and valleys. It was, to say the least, an amazing experience—one that I was so glad I was able to share with my daughter. We saw a vast amount of wildlife, including red foxes, elk, and even a snowy owl. It was the snowy owl that really caught my attention because I can recall a time that my daughter was in fourth grade and had to do a project about the snowy owl. I mean when you see a snowy owl, it's pretty clear how the bird got its name: they're snow white. I came to learn that most owls sleep during the day and hunt at night, but the snowy owl is active during the day, because he's able to camouflage himself to the environment in order to hunt for lemmings—his prey of choice.

It's a known fact in the real estate industry that people trust and work with those who think and act like themselves. This is a security and safety net in the decision-making process, but in fact, there really is no decision at all because our brains always return to what we did yesterday. If it didn't kill us, we repeat the same pattern. But how do we as real estate agents work with the masses if we don't always get along with everyone? We become the snowy owl and blend in, camouflage ourselves with the scenery so that we look, feel, and act like our prospects.

Learning and Understanding Your Prospects

Earlier in my real estate career, I hired a sales coach because I really had no sales experience whatsoever, so in order for me to be on the fast track to becoming the best possible salesperson that I was going to be, I hired a coach from the Sandler Training Institute. I think I googled "sales training coach near me," and the Sandler Institute was in the top five choices. I remember meeting with my coach, and he nurtured me right into the sale so softly and gently. I felt understood in my frustrations as a real estate agent. He listened so attentively to my concerns. I knew I needed this because I didn't have the skill set or the verbiage whatsoever. I mean, I came from a teaching background—the only thing I had ever tried to sell was a game of kickball to thirteen-year-old girls, and I'm sure you could figure out how that went: whomp, whomp. I really felt I needed this because I wanted my goal of making $100k to happen right away. The process of learning the ins and outs of real estate was taking too long. By listening to others in the office, I knew I needed an accountability partner. My Sandler sales coach was an instant fit.

Sandler introduced me to DISC personality profiling, and it was later reinforced in my real estate sales career by Angel

Tucker, a mind-set trainer at EXIT Realty International. The DISC is a behavior assessment tool based on the theory of psychologist William Molton Marstons. It centers on four different personality traits: dominance, influencer, steadiness, and conscientiousness. For example, have you ever given the same listing presentation to potential sellers and each of them had totally different reactions? How can saying the same words produce such different results? Each property owner "heard" you differently based on his or her personality style! You said the same thing, but what they heard was different because each prospect's personality is both naturally and environmentally built into who they are. Different is not bad; it is just different!

Your personality comes from your DNA, the genes given to you by your parents. You can't choose these. And your personality also is a product of your environment: your childhood, the neighborhood you grew up in, and the activities you participated in. For ourselves and others, a lack of understanding of our personalities can often lead to real snags in the selling process, such as tension, disappointment, hurt feelings, unmet expectations, and poor communication. As you know, it is difficult to work with a problem, especially if you do not understand what is going on inside the mind of the client. You see, human behavior, as we all know, can be somewhat of a mystery, whether you're interacting with prospects in the workplace or at home with your children. Think about your significant other and the last argument you had. Did either of you feel misunderstood? Were you able to feel appreciated in your point of view? It's easy to misunderstand our partners' priorities and perspectives, especially when we're quicker to get upset and slower to communicate directly.

While in a transaction with your buyers and sellers, the problem is that miscommunication feeds on itself and we can get caught in a negative cycle of communication that may be difficult to correct. But what if we as real estate salespeople have superhuman powers and could predict behavior? Would you be able to leverage your production? Close more listing appointments and increase your cash flow?

The superhuman power is in the DISC. Once you begin to understand human behavior and see, feel, and hear exactly how your prospect is going to behave next in the sales process, you have gained an advantage. I always knew that people bought from those they liked, so as a sales person, bonding and rapport as well as mirroring behavior was always important, but through DISC, I could see the outcome before my prospect did, I was able to meet them where they were, not where I am in the sales process.

A while back, I was being interviewed by a seller for the sale of his mom's estate home. He showed me around the home, and I asked nurturing questions to diagnose his problem and mirrored his body movements. I could tell right away he was a D/C personality. This personality type blend is a mix of a doer, who is dominant and decisive, as well as cautious, careful and calculating. They are also very task oriented and lack the emotional attachment to people. His job as a person in law enforcement gave it away. So, I got straight to the presentation and led him through it. He appreciated the analysis I diligently explained to him in a rather rapid manner. My challenge was his sister, sitting in on the interview, who was an I/S personality. She was an influencer, very interactive, slightly impulsive, and very people focused in a sincere and stable environment. While being calculating, dominant, and conscientious, I still had to be cognizant of her opposite personality and therefore moved at a slower pace and reexplained the presentation a second time to her, so she would completely understand my marketing plan. To say the least, I was there for over two hours but got the listing because I met them where they were and mirrored both of their personalities.

What I'm trying to get at here is that everyone you encounter is your ideal client—your dentist, kid's teacher, garbage man, and even the checkout girl at the supermarket. Your ideal client is ultimately the property owner. They have the goods, a property, and you provide the service.

My Wave

As you recall earlier in the chapter, before real estate, I worked part time in town for our local parks department. It was a job riddled with a lot of downtime, so I was able to get organized and make some phone calls while on breaks. I let everyone know in that office that I was their go-to real estate agent. In fact, my first sale of a home came from an employee in my office. I was also able to do two rentals my first year in the business to employees in that office. In fact, just the other day, a woman who I still keep in contact with, as our sons are the same age, reached out and said she's looking to purchase her very first home. So, what I'm saying is no matter what background you come from, find a way to leverage your sphere of influence. It just so happens that I've been getting my hair cut by the same person for the last twenty years. He's been listening to me and my real estate stories each and every time I sit in his chair. In the last year, he's listed two homes with me and plans to purchase another. So, it pays to establish relationships with people who you're constantly in contact with.

So how do you effectively use your past positions and careers without coming across as salesy to leverage your sphere of influence?

First, set up your top fifty. These are the fifty people who own property, are in your cell phone contact list that you know will possibly do business with you. It's important to find out if there is another real estate sales agent any of your top fifty may have on their radar should they decide to buy or sell. If you want to be their agent, be ready and willing to help them have their dream come true of either buying or selling a home.

Second, you need to convey that you are there to assist them. You're not there to be a high-pressure salesperson or put them in an uncomfortable situation. It's a matter of having the confidence to convey you want to help them through your business.

Next, I always like sending a text to grab a cup of coffee or a quick bite to eat, not to talk about real estate, but to keep them close in the friends and family zone.

Finally, make sure you have contact information, especially an email, so you're staying in contact with them on a weekly basis. This way when they are ready to buy or sell you are there for them.

As my mentor has always said, "People don't care what you know until they know how much you care." It is a cliché in life and in sales. Before you try to convince your prospects, customers, and sphere of influence or SOI to utilize your service as a real estate agent, they need to first know that you're truly invested in solving their problem. Once your prospect has any inclination that you are coming to them strictly for the extrinsic motivation, money, you lost them. The "What's in It for Me" mentality or WII FM radio station, is a sure way to lose the sale and possibly the customer for life. This is because it is the ego getting involved. The ego is our sense of self or our identity. It perceives life into opposing forces, such as love and hate or good and bad. Showing your prospects and customers that you care is not just about being all mushy and emotional, that's coming from my high D personality type, it's more about being genuine and authentic at every step of the communication process and being a great listener. This means asking questions with inquiry, a curious spirit and truly looking for ways to provide valuable solutions to any challenges that surface. You don't have to have all the answers, but you do have to care enough to seek out the answer to the problem.

At the end of the day, caring about their needs first, and not tuning into WII FM might just lead you to tell a potential customer that you may not be the best agent for them or that a competitor might be a better fit. Either way, people will appreciate your refreshing, honest, and invigorating approach to solving their problem, giving you a better chance to earn their trust and their business down the road or maybe even a referral. In the end it matters how deep the relationship runs.

In essence, I was building a database of my target audience. These are people who are the highest-quality prospects who are going to buy the type of properties that I want to sell. Homeowners are unlimited, which helped me continue to grow.

Closings are happening every day, so I could put in as much work as I wanted to, but you will lose your target audience if you are not present on a consistent basis. The best prospects are the ones who want to work with you now, who have the needs that are fulfilled by your sales service. Not everyone is going to want to work with you and that's OK because you're not going to want to work with everyone either. This puts you in the best position possible and gives you the best chances of working with the best clients. It's kind of like putting your ticket in a prize bag for a charity event. If you put your tickets in a bag numerous times, your chances of getting that prize increase. It's the same thing with homeowners. If you come in contact with as many homeowner prospects as possible, then you have more of a chance to be working with those homeowners when they want to sell their property. Ultimately, talking to homeowners and creating relationships is building your brand. Remember this is You Inc. It's all about you and branding yourself. I know your brokerage is part of your brand, and you will have its logo on your business cards, but you are still your brand; you have your own identity. Your raving fans will follow you like groupies all over the county and state you live in because you are an expert in the field of real estate.

Chapter 7
LIGHT MY WAY—
AUDIOSLAVE

I began real estate in the winter of 2012 as a buyer's agent for my mentor. Now, I have never run a marathon, or a 5K for that matter. Running bores me, but I felt like an antelope in the Serengeti attempting an escape from a starving cheetah. I just kept running and running. I was eager and wanted to learn every aspect of the business. I would volunteer to go to home inspections, drop off contracts, and even manage social media accounts. Now remember, I have no marketing experience whatsoever. My introverted self didn't even have a Facebook page. I was doing all the active, moneymaking activities as well as taking out buyers, running open houses, writing up offers, and prospecting on the phone and by knocking on doors. I was truly my mentor's buyer's agent who would run the buyers from house to house and bring in the offers so she could negotiate back in the office. We really worked well together, and my efforts boosted her business tremendously in the first two years together.

There was a significant amount of growth. It was empowering how free I felt from letting go of the paycheck of my part-time job, but I was exhausted. Running yourself ragged can be counterproductive, as I experienced a dip in my production in year five of my real estate career. I was too exhausted to truly achieve the level of efficiency I was capable of.

Also, at that time, I was working so hard in my business, making a decent amount of income, yet life wasn't harmonious or falling into place. I felt as if I was going crazy over everything. My life felt random, incomplete, and chaotic, so how could my career be successful in chaos? I know I'm smart enough to know what's happening—I have a master's degree for goodness sake—but why am I not able to fix the problem? Why am I consistently frustrated in all my relationships? It seemed as though life was spinning into a vicious pattern like a tornado; cyclic with no clear sunshine in sight.

This problem was costing me a life that I was proud of that I knew I was capable of giving to myself and my family. It was also costing me clients at work because I could not stay focused as my mind was always wondering and fantasizing about the future, focusing on money, and trying so hard to make my clients want to work with me.

I had to figure out a better way. I had to be home more and see my daughter grow up. Because of my absenteeism, I was missing so much, and I didn't realize it until she point-blank told me, "Mommy, you're never home." It crushed my spirit. Destroyed me to the core. Any single ounce of happiness I had in that moment washed over and through my body and was erased with her last word. Bad mom moment? Yes, indeed.

Time blocking became the single most important step in shifting my real estate career. Time blocking is a type of scheduling that can help you manage your time better. Instead of working by the clock, you can focus on finishing big and small tasks one at a time. This will help you limit distractions, get things done faster, and leave you less overwhelmed by lengthy to-do lists It enabled me to get a simple, straightforward and decisive understanding of how to spend my time so that I was able to make every hour of the day productive while minimizing the "busy body tasks," such as organizing my desk, preparing marketing materials, or internet searching, that came to take up mindless space in my brain. Knowing what I should be doing at all times ensured I was staying focused on high-impact, moneymaking activities instead of reacting to everything that popped up and suddenly appeared on my desk.

The "Perfect Week" model was instilled in my brain and on my vision board. Here, I was able to outline the moneymaking activities at each time of the day. I essentially tracked every hour of the day and stuck to a plan. It kept me grounded in my business and it reinforced my purpose.

In 2015, I hired Verl Workman and his staff in response to how chaotic my work-life balance became. He was the one who actually introduced me to time blocking and the Perfect Week model. Thanks to Verl Workman, I ironed out my Perfect Week to fit all my needs and create a balance between work and play. I quickly learned that time blocking enables you to take personal time without feeling guilty or overwhelmed. I saw a change in my attitude and my daughter's behavior quickly after implementing my Perfect Week scheduling. Most importantly, at this this point, I was home when my daughter needed me most to put food on the table. And we began to trade in macaroni and cheese for barbecue chicken.

I filled my perfect workweek with activities that were moneymaking and active in nature such as prospecting, reaching out to my SOI, open houses, listing appointments, buyer appointments, and previewing homes. I also included passive activities, such as office work, role playing, education, and administrative tasks. And then there was also gym time and home time. Each of these was no less important than the other as they created a steadiness and equal footing for my life with a holistic approach. It also allowed me to be more deliberate in my path to reach my goals. Now, I knew I was on to something here as I felt a pressure and burden lift almost immediately.

The second shift in my approach to my real estate career came with the discovery of the book *You Inc: The Art of Selling Yourself*, by Harry Beckwith and Christine Clifford. The book is composed of mostly small, easy-to-do commonsense tips for salespeople, but when combined and utilized in a complete package, it could result in amazing alterations in your career as a salesperson. No matter what good product or service is being sold, the most important component in the sale is *you*. You are the procuring cause of any real estate transaction. And without *you* there is no transaction, no deal, and no commission. When in sales, these changes shift your mind-set so that you treat yourself as a business entity. Mic drop!

Another mentor, Rick O'Neil, always talked about *You Inc.* and how we as real estate agents should treat ourselves as a business. After all, we brand ourselves, market our services, and invest in ourselves, and the people buy and sell through us. Of course! That's how we become the most popular person in the neighborhood—the Rock star real estate agent.

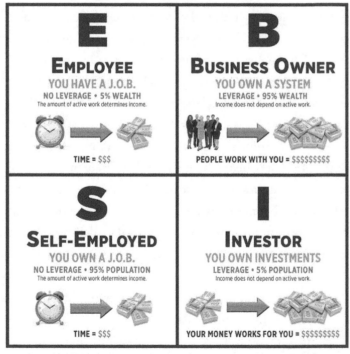

CASHFLOW QUADRANT
4 WAYS TO PRODUCE INCOME
LINEAR INCOME VS. LEVERAGED & RESIDUAL INCOME

E

EMPLOYEE
YOU HAVE A J.O.B.
NO LEVERAGE • 5% WEALTH
The amount of active work determines income.

TIME = $$$

B

BUSINESS OWNER
YOU OWN A SYSTEM
LEVERAGE • 95% WEALTH
Income does not depend on active work.

PEOPLE WORK WITH YOU = $$$$$$$$$

S

SELF-EMPLOYED
YOU OWN A J.O.B.
NO LEVERAGE • 95% POPULATION
The amount of active work determines income.

TIME = $$$

I

INVESTOR
YOU OWN INVESTMENTS
LEVERAGE • 5% POPULATION
Income does not depend on active work.

YOUR MONEY WORKS FOR YOU = $$$$$$$$$

Most of us are familiar with the upper left quadrant as we have been trained or conditioned to be employees.
Being an employee or self-employed makes for about 95%of the population and it creates a huge dependency...**Ourselves**.

I devoured the book *Rich Dad, Poor Dad*, by Robert Kiyosaki and got swept up in the cash flow quadrant: employee, self-employed, business owner, investor. As real estate agents, we are all working in the S quadrant, but I have to be honest. I really didn't want to be in the S quadrant. Our names are our business, after all; if I'm a business, shouldn't I be receiving all the great tax benefits of owning a business? That's when my LLC was born and registered.

Utilizing myself as a business organization meant I was the broker. I was a brokerage inside of a brokerage. I put together an onboarding manual with job descriptions, policy, and procedures and started implementing QuickBooks for all my accounting. My plan was to build a team of agents; showing agents, buyer's agents, listing agents, and an administrator. It was this sense of ownership that kept me grounded. I was responsible for building this business I was creating—a pathway to wealth for my business—and the pursuit began. I went back and revised my listing presentation as well. The pathway to growth seemed much clearer.

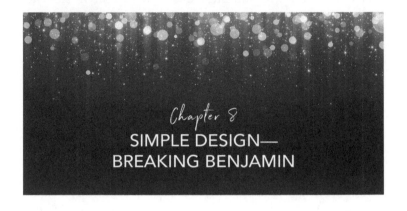

Chapter 8

SIMPLE DESIGN—
BREAKING BENJAMIN

I can recall teaching bow-and-arrow skills to a junior high class in Wyoming. Now, I was a city girl from New York and had no clue how to shoot a bow and arrow—not one iota—but I was determined to learn the skill and understand it so that I could competently teach it to my students. Now I could have just haphazardly picked up a book and read it from front to back and examined the pictures in detail about format and precise release and grip, but I didn't. I had to actually physically do the tasks and execute the lead up skills. This doesn't mean I didn't fail. Oh, I failed miserably. So much so that I nearly quit. But I knew it was a skill my students would appreciate given the environment they lived in. I had to go through the uncomfortable process and release my fears and anxiety of the new skill I was learning. Extremely difficult given my D (doer) personality.

Goals need to be deeper than money. Money is never the goal. It can be a part of it, but it should never be the end all or the result. This is why I stayed off social media for a year. The images and pressure of society to meet goals was crushing me, destroying my morale, and making me think that I wasn't good enough, earning enough, or designing the elite life that I wanted to live—at least, not by the standards of my family, friends, or society.

I started asking myself why am I trying to reach my goals? What makes me move forward? Why do I get up in the morning and walk into my office? Why was I so determined to make $100k? Hmmmm.

I was then introduced to Simon Sinek after the broker owner training for my company. I was awestruck, and that doesn't usually happen with me. Now if you've never heard of Simon, he is the author of *Start with Why*. His book was inspirational. I found happiness and fulfillment in the *Why* discovery process. And doing it with another person makes it easier to discover your why for your own personal growth. It's not what you do that matters it's *why* you do it. Discovering your why serves as a tool to build and inspire those around you, but it can be difficult to find and see.

Your *Why*, or your purpose, is a pattern or theme within your story. These behaviors are the times in your life that you were most fulfilled and genuinely happy, which reveals the makeup of your *Why*. Your *Why* is your emotions, feelings, values, and beliefs, which come from the limbic brain. Yet language, the words to express your emotions, come from the neocortex part of the brain. This presents a challenge. Finding your *Why* is a rational process where you think you have the answer so you want to share it, but it can be difficult to express it because of the areas of your brain that it comes from. It's just biology.

I never saw my *Why* as providing for my family. It went much deeper than putting steak on the table, wanting a better lifestyle, or seeing my daughter go to college. To me, those are still superficial. I dug deeper, harder, really searched my core to find my meaning, my purpose in life. Reaching down to my inner child to find the happiest times of my life. It was more like asking myself what is my mission, why am I here? It's a matter of getting crystal clear on what's driving you, bringing purpose to your life and what's worth fighting for. This will become your motivation for where you are going and where you want to be. Finding your *Why* is finding the thing that keeps you motivated.

I found I was happiest when I was playing a sport and part of a team. As an athlete, I belonged to something that was greater than me. My teammates pushed me to a level unlike one I could ever have achieved on my own. We couldn't win the game unless we could cooperate, combine forces, and win games. My goals without the support of my teammates were not achievable. My success was dependent on others. Yes, the mentality was a bit codependent, but I couldn't fail. I would never allow the defeatist mentality to sucker me into the depths I could not get out of. When I found my mission and my purpose as a team member, I was living a much happier and, in essence, better life. By joining forces and connecting to those with likeness and similarities, I made a pretty powerful discovery.

In my *Why* discovery, I found joy and pleasure in connecting to a higher purpose and moral responsibility and obligation to be obedient to God in his quest for me. This helped me live a financially freeing life in which I am able to provide an abundant lifestyle for my family. This was my difference in the world. I kept it present with me every day: it was the first thing I read in the morning and the last thing I read at night.

How was this relevant to real estate? Those who I surrounded myself with were the influencers of how I performed in real estate, including my coaches, mentors, and broker. I found a church leader to speak with on a weekly basis, connected with members of my women's groups for coffee and sought out inspirational *Mastermind* retreats from some of the most influential leaders for personal growth. These were women entrepreneurs making high six-figure incomes in their business. My vision or purpose in real estate and life was so clear and became my mantra. "Surround yourself with the best people who also have a mission to lead with purpose" is something that gave me continuous energy to invest my time and spirit into beautiful, life-changing experiences deeply rooted in connecting to those around me. Connect, connect, connect at a deep level. Find your community, your tribe, your family, your culture! Martin Rutte, author of *Chicken Soup for the Soul*, calls this finding your Heaven on Earth. So, are you living with purpose or is it lying still and silent deep inside you?

Your purpose is right there in front of you just waiting to be discovered with your own eyes. There are signs pointing you toward your purpose and your own why and meaning of life. It's a matter of finding the courage and faith to follow the signs that are there. Finding meaning is a matter of following your faith and heart, letting go of all the doubt and negativism surrounding you, staying present in the moment and understanding that there are no coincidences. You are meant to be here at this moment reading this book, on this page right here and right now. Following your greater good will soon become clear, and it will help guide you to your purpose and your why.

Soon you will find yourself speaking up to ending bad business relationships and deciding not to work with clients because they are just not a good fit with your real estate philosophy because following your heart is more natural and pleasing. It will create an ease filled with peace and harmony in your business.

Simply doing the right thing might be risky to some extent, dangerous to your real estate business, and you might even lose a few deals out of it; your fear will show its ugly face as anxiety and lack of control from deals that are not happening. Most real estate agents give in to the money, and don't get me wrong, money does have a place in the world. But when you follow your heart, the money will follow, giving you the passion, energy, and motivation to overcome the most difficult transactions, the most difficult bosses, and the most difficult clients. The obstacles in your way will effortlessly be hurdled. You will notice a fire deep inside you pushing you to limits you never thought were possible. Following your heart relaxes all parts of the body, releasing all tension.

Next, discovering my *Why* included reaching a self-actualization level of my own personal needs. It has become a matter of getting wiser and humbler in business where the client and I have had a natural flow and movement through the transaction as I guide them along the way. In many ways, the real estate business is a transcendence of personal growth that has fulfilled me in my own personal quest for happiness. So, I challenge you to think about why you went into real estate?

Where do you see yourself in one, three, or five years?

What life do you want to live?

I have always been obsessed with growing and educating myself internally. I can't stand sitting still—it bores me beyond belief. Challenging myself is a rush of adrenaline—my fix and vice. This quest and force inside me drove me to find my passion, allowing for a liberating freedom in my real estate business— one of living without fear. As a result of my never-ending quest, I emerged wiser and better and transformed myself to be the person I was meant to be with a clear, focused picture filled with clarity and meaning.

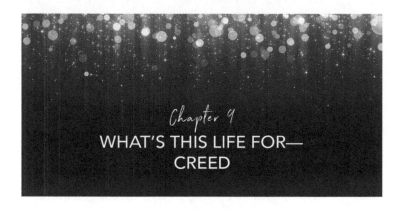

ouldn't it be nice to open up the office door today and
know that you're getting a listing agreement signed,
your buyer client is making a full-price offer and you're
going to have a deal in contract form by 5:00 p.m., your kid
gets a 100 on his or her math test, and your love interest is
ready to take the next step with you? It's the door that leads to
every CEO's need, want, desire, and ability to run a Fortune

500 company. What if I told you you have the same talent! You are more than capable of leading a dynamic real estate business filled with the closings happening every day! You already possess such a gift. It was given to you before you were born, before you even thought about going into real estate to earn some hustle money, and it's as simple as turning the key to open the door for that 2:00 p.m. open house.

The key to assessing your potential lies with you. You must understand the choices you made in your real estate career to hold on to or let go of your part-time paycheck, to work on a Saturday, sacrifice time with family, and to miss your kid's field day event have made you who you are today. And it's OK that this has happened in the past. You may even be feeling some guilt and disappointment. As long as you are not imprisoned by your stories through self-gratifying behavior, reacting to rather than responding to uncomfortable situations or overindulging in sex, drugs, food, and alcohol (you thought I was gonna say rock-and-roll), we can learn how to create new empowering stories. You're in this spot in your real estate career right now, reading this book at this time, because you're meant to be here—*now*!

The real estate market and property owners need real estate agents like you who are filled with a life force and energy that is limitless in reaching your potential. Agents that care create a space to restore personal power within themselves.

Physically Fit for Success

Giving birth to my daughter was one of the more difficult things for me to do. I was in labor for four days with two- to three-minute contractions the whole time. So, what could be more difficult than that? Losing the forty pounds I had gained. And more difficult than that? Keeping it off for good.

I would lose and gain playing the yo-yo game for several years on multiple fad diets. I dabbled in Jenny Craig, counted my points with Weight Watchers, and got sick as dog on the Atkins diet before the keto diet was all the rage. My background in health and fitness provided me with basic insight, as I knew the food I was eating was influencing what I looked like physically. Being fifty pounds overweight was not the best look for a thirty-nine-year-old single mom, let alone a real estate agent giving multiple presentations to various people. What did they think looking at me this way? How could I be confident and give a great presentation when the clothes I'm wearing are too tight because the mac and cheese I've been eating is literally attaching itself to my hips and tush (my ZZ top reference)? I felt disgusting. I was uninspired to roll out of bed, to go to work, to huff and puff walking up second-floor stairs of a colonial home I would be showing, and I couldn't wear the cute and sexy ninety-dollar heels I had bought myself after last week's closing.

The simplistic thing that you can start doing today without any huge disruption in your patterns is increasing your water intake. Water has many benefits for how your blood flows through your blood stream, which increases your oxygen distribution throughout the body. So, if you're feeling tired or have a headache, don't reach for the coffee drink instead get a glass or two of water. You're most likely dehydrated. It should be the first thing you do in the morning after a night's sleep of perspiring—especially, for women beginning menopause.

In the United States, we are spending so much money on healthcare, and it's the pharmaceutical companies that are growing rich. The healthcare system was designed to care for illness, disease, and cancer. And all of these conditions have been proven to come from the imbalance of the gut. That's why "you are what you eat" is so very true and a primary principal that we should be listening to. I can recall listening to a podcast with Naveen Jain. In it, he reinforces this simple concept about how the organisms in your gut have a huge impact on our health. Your metabolism can be optimized by taking care of your gut bacteria. So, eating whole, clean, healthy foods is so important to your real estate performance. It's not just about what we look like, as we are the presenters to our raving fans, but how we feel inside and what's occurring in our bodies. I said previously in this chapter you are what you eat, which influences how you feel. How one feels inside one's body can translate into presenting better to prospects and being received better by them. Our health impacts our well-being. Check out David Asbury and his fitness transformation. Whoa!

Through EXIT Realty International founder Steve Morris, I was led to *Eating for Your Blood Type*, by Dr. Peter Adamo. Through the extension of the research of his father, Dr. Adamo, he outlines the food we should and should not be eating and which foods are harmful and healthy based on the blood type we are. He continues to say there are huge benefits in following the eating plan of your blood type where one can see massive health benefits of simple, whole food nutrition with supplement and interval training activity. This all dates back to our ancestors and our native origins. For instance, I am blood type O (being positive or negative is irrelevant). O blood type are known to have a strong immune and digestive system as well as an efficient metabolism that is hardy against illness. The blood type O are the original meat-eating ancestors and therefore do much better with a diet high in protein. We do best with red meat and fish and should avoid turkey at all costs. Green leafy vegetables, broccoli and fruits like apricot, blueberries, and pineapple.

Gyms and pressing weights are not my thing, but I kept with the 80/20 rule. What you look like and how you feel is 80 percent eating habits and 20 percent workout plan. I chose to focus on the 80 percent and roll the dice with the other

20 percent. I increased my step climbing efforts in showing properties and would park my car down the block as opposed to right in front of the property.

I now had clarity on a more scientific-based approach to health and fitness that made sense. My master's degree was nothing compared to the education I received in my self-health discovery. It was so primitive yet so eye opening and encouraging reading about the basics of health as opposed to listening to a 2 a.m. infomercial. By eating clean, drinking more water, and doing some intermittent fasting, I was able to shed the baby weight and keep it off.

As the weight fell off, I was sleeping better and became more productive. My reflexes were faster, I had better responses to objections and the boringness of administrative paperwork was complete by the end of a workday. Additionally, I had more energy to invest in my daughter and her activities.

The Three M's

My head space seemed clearer, but not totally. I joined a women's support group for single moms to become surrounded by like-minded people, and what they all had in common besides the obvious was the practice of the three M's: mindfulness, meditation, and manifesting. What the heck did I just join? But I was open to listening as their sharing resonated with my own painful experiences.

Mindfulness is bringing awareness into the present moment and taking a breath as a discipline to deal with stress in the right now is so important for us as real estate agents. How many times has a client said something to cause a disruption in the flow of your day? This is a matter of taking a deep breath to feel better and stay calm. It's an amusing guided visualization to redirect your focus to the present moment. There are many apps and YouTube videos out there to help with mindfulness.

Now my preconceived notion of meditation was monks closing their eyes and humming on carpets for hours in silence. I could be disturbed by any wind, a bird chirping, or my child saying, "Mommy, what's for dinner?" My undiagnosed ADD has no patience to sit still for anything for hours at time. And as a real estate agent, the constant ringing of my cell phone, whistling of a text message, and email dings would not allow me to shut off. But these women seemed calm and patient, and they expressed how through meditation they were able to disconnect from the world yet still be more present in the moment. The world was clear, and they could focus on tasks.

Meditation is a fourth state of consciousness where the areas of the brain that hold the past and present talk to each other in unison. Therefore, the whole brain is firing on all eight cylinders creating changes within the brain itself. The ability of the brain to change itself is called neuroplasticity. By developing new connections and pruning away weak ones, the brain is able to adapt to the changing environment. There are incredible changes that occur in the brain as a result of meditation. Besides being more focused are sure to experience exponential creativity and untapped talents, being present in your relationships and super healing powers. Melissa Fletcher is a great educator and speaker on this subject.

I can recall negotiating a deal with a co-agent from my office. It was pretty intense as neither one of us was backing off our client's demands, but for the good of the office we wanted to work it out. This debate was heated, and I walked away from it physically and mentally exhausted. I took my little knowledge of meditation, which meant playing a YouTube video, and went with it. It was a guided meditation to cleanse my ego. What I experienced was a rush through my body. It was an enthralling invigoration, like on a roller coaster, yet calming at the same time, but on a spiritual level. I had awakened from a deep-cleansing sleep on a totally different, new level than what I got from regular sleep. At the time, I could only describe it a as a deep, healing sleep. But what it was actually doing was healing not only the stresses in the present moment, such as being on time to appointments, meeting the demands of clients, and what nutritious meal I was putting on the table for dinner, but also those deep, awful resonating stresses of the past. The stresses of trauma from childhood and not getting my needs met from the child-parent relationship. They were being cleansed, scrubbed, and erased from my cellular memory, just like a computer.

Fletcher says, "Stress makes you stupid." I love this saying. It makes you sick and slow. And your doctor could probably confirm he's seeing more stress-related illness now than ever before. This is why it's super important to live a stress-free life, not only to be healthy, but also to make decisions for yourself and your business.

Manifesting Your Desires

The fast-food industry has changed since the days of Burger King's "Have It Your Way" ads. Other establishments such as Subway, Starbucks, and Chipotle have joined the "me generation" to create individual choices when it comes to your food order. I get so nervous in these types of establishments, as it sends my undiagnosed ADD into disarray because you to be very intentional and specific when ordering.

"I'll take a large black coffee."

Is that a venti or a grande?

Milk or cream?

Equal or cane sugar?

What? I just want a large coffee.

Placing every order is individualistic to the hunger or thirst desires of the customer. That's kind of how manifesting works. There's no set subject to manifest, but you have to set the right intention and be purposeful when requesting your desire. You must know why you want what you want. This can be a magical experience where your thoughts become things. So, can you make $100k in real estate? Do you believe it's possible that you can earn $100k from real estate? Are you internally fulfilled earning $100k in real estate?

Balancing Spiritualism with Professional Hustle

Using a more Eastern approach and the universe to create a more holistic and natural approach to health, wellness, food, and fitness did seem a little unnatural at first, but I did welcome it, especially if improvements in my real estate business were going to occur. Heck, I was almost willing to try anything for that to happen. But, being raised Catholic made me quite uneasy. I felt as though I was betraying God's place in my life. That's when I started to question God's role in my life and in my business.

The real estate world is filled with many self-indulgent and ego-driven agents and brokers with their hands out looking for money at every open door. As an agent, the real estate business tested my morals, values, and how to be a godly and righteous person who is humble and serving out of the goodness of her heart. It was disheartening to see transactions die because of selfishness. Could God actually have a place in real estate transactions?

As a result of being cutthroat and conforming to the operations of most real estate agents, I was at a low point in my career. It had been months since my last closing, and the highs and lows of my real estate closings were in a deep canyon. I was depressed. It was difficult most days to even get out of bed. My mind-set was pessimistic, and I couldn't focus on completing simple tasks like making dinner. I definitely burned a few dinners back then. My chicken dinners, and sometimes steak on Saturdays, were on the verge of going back to mac and cheese. I couldn't close a deal.

I was still attending my weekly women's meeting because there was a vibrancy after the two hours of opening myself up to others and sharing from experience. I always felt invigorated, rejuvenated and alive at the closing of each meeting as if something had taken over my soul. I had peaceful hours of sleep without being awakened at night or having to take an over the counter medication to relax me to sleep. My journals revealed I performed better the next day at the office as well. These meetings refreshed my spirit of God's role in my business and ultimately my life.

I centered myself by beginning an intimate relationship with God and began a spirit-led business filled with love, joy, peace, patience, kindness, goodness, and faithfulness. And that's just what I started to become: sincere in my intentions, humbler in my acceptance of a commission, and committed to the clients I was serving.

This wasn't an overnight altered state of awareness. It was a period of growth that unraveled and revealed itself when I was ready for it. I had to sacrifice a part of myself, the par that was used to hustling and grinding harder than anyone else, to give in to my spiritual core. And whether you believe in God, the universe, or something else, in order to create the real estate career you desire, letting go of control, of the attachment, in order to be guided through your words and actions allows you to be free and surrender. In turn, new opportunities and experiences will begin to present themselves, and key business relationships will arrive when you weren't even looking because you were blinded by obstacles.

With so much destruction happening in the world today, it's amazing how the real estate market is still spinning and making the world go round and around using its same traditional methods.

Your dream life will manifest itself, and you will begin creating the life you desire. So, start letting go of that which does not serve your real estate career and start loving the real estate life and its multiple avenues. It's then that your true desires will have a voice. The freedom will open you up to let go of anger and have more gratitude in your life.

Chapter 10
MONEY TALKS—
AC/DC

*M*y goal in real estate was always to make $100k a year. I figured if I could do that then I would be able to keep putting chicken on the table and quit working my steady-paying part-time job getting a biweekly paycheck. But I quickly realized that was never going to happen. I had tried to be everything to everyone, make everyone around me was happy while I was sacrificing myself to meet the needs of those

I served. The hurdle was finding the time to service my clients the way they deserved to be serviced. It was nearly impossible to play mommy, town employee, and real estate agent all in the same day without mental and physical fatigue. I thought it would be easy; after all, I had been watching my mother do it as a single parent for twenty years. Earlier, you'll remember, I talked about going into real estate with a moneymaking mindset focusing on the deal, forcing the transaction, and at times even obsessing about every single detail of the transaction and how it became an all-consuming endeavor and was ruining my health and body in the process.

I would see new listings posted in the MLS of interviews I had gone on a week before with a homeowner and would get so freaking pissed I didn't get the listing. I remember one time leaving the office and *sitting in my car in the parking lot* crying, feeling betrayed, abandoned, and all alone. I mean, I sat down with this homeowner, shared a Sprite with him, and he was now just leaving me in the dark to put mac and cheese back on the table for my daughter. It ruined my day sometimes to the point where I would take my frustration out on those closest to me. My daughter got the brunt of every missed listing to put it harshly.

I can recall thinking, "Why didn't this homeowner like me? Why am I not good enough? How come they are not using me to sell their home? It consumed my mind and depressed me, creating this "woe is me" mind-set and funk that was extremely difficult to get out of.

I always thought if I only had more experience, more time under my belt, they would like me more and they would hire me in an instant, just like Mom. I saw my mother do all of it on her own as a single mother and figured I could do the same right? *Wrong!* After all, she was extremely successful. Everywhere we went, people recognized her. This was all in part of her branding herself and her name. She was like the neighborhood real estate guru. When we went food shopping or if we went to the local community festival, someone would recognize her. I mean, her name was even on the back of a T-shirt for a local event she sponsored.

But what I didn't understand at the time was it wasn't just the branding and marketing of herself through all these platforms, she was also consciously able to talk to people and invite them into her circle of trust. Everywhere we went, real estate was happening, and she managed to take those conversations at basketball games, the mall, or the changing a flat tire and turn them into business.

I didn't get the gift of gab to be social and talk. Mom always said that of all four of her kids, I was the last one she thought would go into real estate because I wasn't as social as the others. But I was very observant of social situations, studying people constantly. My introverted self can be cautious at times. Some call it shy, but I was an eternal student always looking to grow. Everyone believed I would probably not be so successful in real estate. And hearing those words and seeing those pessimistic and negative attitudes toward me made me want to prove them wrong. My focus was all over the place until my light bulb went on.

At my daughter's softball games, I like to sit in the outfield far, far away from the chaos and drama that happens behind home plate and the dugout. So, I quietly enjoy the joys of parenting and being proud of my child from a distance. I find it to be the most relaxing part of parenting.

Additionally, she's a great horseback rider, and I keep away from the ring there as well. At a horse show some years ago, a parent overheard me talking to a client about a transaction. Our kids had played together and hung out for years in and out of the horse show ring, we had gone to church and ate dinners together, and we shared horse stories about our kids riding. We had become good friends. Then one day while our kids were riding out in the ring together, we got to talking.

"You're in real estate right?" She asked me.

I responded, "Well, yes I am."

"My husband is looking to sell his childhood home, we are looking to sell our home nearby, and we want to purchase a horse property so we can stop paying these boarding fees. Can you help me?"

Aha. Light bulb.

"Well, yes. Of course I can."

At the time, again, I just saw dollar signs, but what this parent saw was trust. We had bonded and created rapport over our mutual sharing and the back and forth that parents do. As a teacher, I also had to provide this trust for the students I taught. They had to trust me to teach them correctly. It was instilled through the system to trust your teacher, but as a real estate salesperson that trust was actually more like a "There's no way in heck I'm trusting a salesperson. Those people are greedy!" So, I did have the skills and the tools to give awesome service to clients, I just couldn't see it and was in my own way because I was focusing on the money and not diving deep into the person sitting in front of me. I was not allowing myself to invest in them while they were giving me their time and investing in me. I kept thinking the more time I "waste" on people, the more money I make. It's OK to sacrifice time to spend with a client, but it can't throw you off doing all your moneymaking activities.

Some years ago, I was hustling hard, focusing all my efforts and energy on one client in the luxury market. This client consumed me from sunup to sundown and even late into the night with text messages and phone calls. After working with him awhile, I soon had psychic abilities about when he was calling. This potential four-million-dollar sales commission was the carrot dangling in front of me and my motivation to slide right to pick up the phone as opposed to hitting the "Forget You" button. But I could feel that large commission check in my hands and a fourteen-day cruise in the Panama Canal.

After months of finessing this client, showing him properties, answering his wee-hour morning calls, and getting a deal accepted and a fully executed contract, I started planning my Panama attire. But then the deal we had fell apart in escrow, and he disappeared—nowhere to be found. Calling this a bad break-up was putting it lightly. This rejection sent me out of the real estate game for a good month. I had a deep lack of motivation. My ego was seriously bruised, and I couldn't focus on the simplest of tasks, let alone find future business

My purpose in telling this story is if we focus on the results, then disappointment will happen, but it's imperative to have the mind-set to get back on track and focus on the day to day actions. It's easy to stay focused on the disappointment, but it's about being in the right frame of mind and focusing on the relationship rather than the end result or the money of the deal. Up until this point, I was focusing on the deals and what was in it for me and not my client. I didn't care anything about the people, and if I did, I could have been closing more deals.

I became excited and pushed and continued on. The real estate work and grind of twelve-hour workdays became easier and felt shorter with this mind-set change. By focusing on the relationships, my emotional real estate card began to show itself. I was able to open my heart little by little and give my prospects a little bit more of myself as well. I was adapting to the market and it was this what forced me to figure out what works and what doesn't.

I began to give the homeowners choices. Just what they wanted. I developed a presentation that met their needs, not mine, in their process and met them at their level. I was kind of like a doctor listening to their pains and woes about third and current homes and asked more and more questions. Who, what, where, when, why, how, in what time? The prospects appreciated it more and more, and buyer customers were turning into buyer clients because they trusted I was doing the right things for them –not for me and my pocket.

Listening was the key to everything. In the past, I was holding back information hoping the homeowner would sign my contract and would pay me later. I didn't have to hold back and be scared of giving too much information. I could tell the prospect everything, which was natural for me. It was my new philosophy in moving forward. It freed me of any expectation from myself and the prospect. I went into every presentation with my new frame of mind and began a new walk of life in real estate. A proud new approach and not one tied in forcing the sale and making the prospect do what they didn't want to do and choose.

The old-school real estate scripts I had learned we're just that—old! They're a handicap. They need to be set on fire along with songs like Guns and Roses "Sweet Child O' Mine" and Bon Jovi's "Cowboy." Those scripts weren't "begging sellers to work with me"; they were actually causing them to run away. Sellers felt handcuffed and forced to make decisions so that I could make money.

My new scripts were light easy breezy; they were just conversations. I didn't need to force any communication because it was happening naturally in a constant flow and rhythm

Next, I needed to have a keener sense of the marketplace. I began having those street conversations, which were very casual and sounded something like: "Hi, my name is Jennifer, and I am a real estate agent. Is there anything I can do to help you out regarding buying and selling real estate?" Most replied with a no, but that was OK. I was still able to get their email and keep them in my weekly drip email campaign, such as Constant Contact or MailChimp. After all, God gave us two ears and one mouth for a reason, and I was listening to him.

My real estate business steadily increased and helped me spread a message through the community that I was there to help people with their needs. I realized that to make more money, I had to invest in my emotional self first and then listen to people. This meant always caring for the person in front of you, showing a deep interest in their words. It meant sending a personal "Thank you" card or remembering a birthday with a gift. My gratitude for having a neighbor in my life was the real key.

By contacting property owners through my neighborhood prospecting, I was able to find new relationships and build a pipeline for future business to happen. This helped me stay in touch with them for a long period of time until they were ready to make a real estate move, buy, sell, or rent a home. I was able to create lifelong relationships with property owners in the neighborhood. I was winning the market just by helping people, knowing the market, and talking real estate. Me talking? Really? No more shy girl.

My real estate message was coming from my heart and not my pocket or lack of money in it. It was a message that resonated with my prospects who needed me most—a client-first philosophy. I was able to structure their problem in their own words and win their trust. Then, I was there at their kitchen table to offer them a real estate marketing plan to help solve their problem so they could move onto the next phase of their life without disruption and chaos. By going deep with my prospects, I was able to transform my business. Referrals were being made, I was getting repeat clients, and a new source of business investors and builders were flocking to me for REO and short sale properties.

I was able to figure out the code and the words that created a substance to create unlimited business. It all starts with four simple words: "How can I help you?"

I sensed and finally came to grips that I couldn't control others' actions and choices or the actions or choices of the property owners. I can only control me and my actions. Caring about my prospects' well-being set me apart from those twenty-year experienced and seasoned agents, and it has helped me surpass them as well.

Chapter 11
UNCHAINED—
VAN HALEN

*R*eal estate can become a place where you can find new inspiration and motivation to move past the things that are holding you back, so that you can create a real estate business and a life you love. This is a practical approach to overcoming fear and that means you must first identify what your fear looks like. For this, we go to Ruth Soupkup.

Conquering Fear

In her book, *Do It Scared: Finding the Courage to Face Your Fears, Overcome Adversity, and Create a Life You Love*, she identifies seven fear archetypes, seven unique ways that fear plays out in people's lives and manifests itself in one's life. The fear archetypes help us identify our own fear patterns. It's not until you can see your own behavior patterns that you can then start to know how to overcome your personal fears. Identifying your fear is the first step in conquering it.

I remember being eight years old and hearing my parents fight about money—what bill was paid and which ones weren't, who charged what on the credit card, and why there was less money than yesterday in the bank account. There was a lot of yelling going on, and it's really my first recollection of hearing what the strains of money can cause in a relationship. It subconsciously stayed with me.

As real estate agents, we have to understand the client's finances in order to service them properly and give them the best first experience. In interviewing buyers, I had to figure out if they were qualified to purchase, so then came the questions like "How much of your savings are you working with?" Cringe. I could feel myself sink in my chair and my face begin to wrinkle as my eyes squinted in anticipation for the buyer to start yelling at me, just like my parents had done when I was eight years old.

As real estate agents, there may be times when we have to find the strength and courage to do hard things to focus on the relationship with the client and give him the best experience. This means we may have to adopt a new set of core beliefs and the mind-set to ask the difficult questions. But how do you stop thinking about all of your fears and having your everyday business consumed by these inner childhood fears? How do you take action if you have been doing it the same way since you were eight years old and probably younger?

Taking action is the key to this puzzle. It's the first remedy in soothing your fears. Taking action is ultimately a practical approach to getting unstuck and moving forward, even if you don't know where the road is going to lead you. This first step is really the hardest and a very basic law of nature. Even Newton's laws of motion can confirm this:

"A body at rest stays at rest, and a body in motion stays in motion unless acted upon by another force."

Very practical in real estate. Here's how.

You wake up with the best of intentions, starting your real estate day at 8:30 a.m. having the best of intentions to make the two hours of cold calls and speak to one hundred people and get four listing appointments. You do this three days a week because it's on your block plan calendar. It's written there in black and white what you have to do to be successful—what your moneymaking activities are. But what do you do?

Answer your emails and reorganize your desk. Why? Because you are hardwired not to change, to keep repeating the same patterns that didn't cause you harm the day before and the day before that.

Our brains like returning to safety. It's natural for us, and our electrical parts do not like taking action. Change creates a state of interruption from the normal routine. This means if you change a particular pattern, behavior, or situation, you become fearful of the outcome, of the unknown. Our brains do not like the pattern interruption. And this is why we don't pick up the phone and make some excuse that our desk is too dirty to make calls. By staying safe in our patterns, our goals and dreams will never come true.

The truth is we all have fear. It's a natural born occurrence for us to have distress. Fear was developed as a part of our natural evolution to keep us safe and alive. But some of these same fears, which are innate, are useless today in our world. There's no reason for us to fear being eaten alive by lions. Yet they still hold us back from being the person we were meant to be.

Some would say go toward your fear! Go through it. Push through it. You can do it. We all know being scared is a transition period and very natural, but it still holds us back. And you're not alone. "Just do it" is difficult and easier said than done. We do not want to suppress our fear because it will manifest itself as anger, frustration, anxiety, and greed. It can cloud judgment and keep you in a trance and paralyze you.

So, how do you find the courage to take action to overcome fear and set things in motion and overcome the negative mindset? It's a matter of finding a catalyst to change and to take the steps for change. For me that catalyst was my complicated rock-and-roll-esque love story. It was willed with unhealthy patterns of self-sabotaging behaviors, like falling in love too quickly and then my partner not meeting my needs, which would lead into the flames dying and the relationship ending. It makes for a great rock song, like the song by Shinedown, "The Crow and the Butterfly." Then there is nothing that can stop you from being truly happy—nothing to stop you from succeeding and achieving your dreams. So, it's more than just facing fears. These are goals that push you past your current limits. It's a matter of pushing past your norms and what you are capable of to get excitement and energy. This creates an unimaginable belief system in which you can fire up your mind to think big. These stretch goals push you past your comfort zone, in which you believe in your capabilities. Settling for anything less is just that—settling, which doesn't require any stretching, changing, or interrupting of patterns. So why should you work harder?

It is your power to choose courage and to overcome fear, which makes you fearless. There is no power in fear. If you follow your heart to goodness, morals, and high standards and have the faith to believe in your higher power whether that's God, the universe, or another deity, this belief will provide you with faith to follow your heart and drive you to go further than you have ever gone before.

Big stretch goals set the stage to get big things done. And those butterflies, the ones that freak us out a bit in our stomachs, are good indicators to move us to go into the unknown. Without these big goals, we are just traveling along aimlessly as society determines the path we should be taking. So, what are your biggest dreams in life? Are they friends, family, money, or work? It doesn't matter—go ahead and allow yourself to really dream big! It's OK to give yourself permission to really envision the life you were meant to live and then commit to it, write it down, put it on your vision board, and start talking about it to everyone who will listen.

And once you get clear about all those big goals and dreams, you need a plan of action. This is where most people get stuck. Technology has given us the "what's most urgent mentality," where we tackle the tasks that feel most important right now. So, attending to your emails and reorganizing your desk may seem important in the present, but they do not align with the bigger picture. But your natural inclination returns you to whatever feels normal and safe in the moment. So, it's a matter of creating a big picture funnel. This is a matter of breaking down your goals into smaller bits and pieces in which there is conscious effort put forth that creates a clear, concise strategy for obtaining your goals.

Holding Yourself Accountable

Next, find those who will hold you accountable for your actions. This is where you will seek out those who will speak the truth to you and push you to grow to be your true authentic self. It's a matter of surrounding yourself with those who will push you to be the best version of you. This could be with a coach who is waiting for you, one where you can be you without judgment, where you can be authentic and real but still held accountable when the moment presents itself. But it's up to you to search them out and find them. That may mean stepping outside your small "circle of trust" in order to make new friends and acquaintances with shared fears, attending a seminar or meeting, so they will inspire you do what it takes to become limitless.

It's in this manner that you regain control over your stagnant real estate business because otherwise you are comparing yourself to the other ten top-producing agents who are crushing the market. The comparison trap, like on social media, can suck you into this mind-set of being trapped and wrapped up in a false reality. "Keeping up with the Joneses" will keep you financially bound and gagged to societal pressures. And if you look around at what everyone else is doing, you will only feel unfulfilled in your parenting, clothing, cars, and even relationships. There's always someone else doing it better than you are. So, stop looking at others and their status because it will only create less success in your own life. Making for a less satisfying life. Success is unique to each person. Your success is personal to you and only you, and it will not be meaningful to others. So, figure out what success looks like for you and you only. Then, become a thoroughbred racehorse at the Belmont Stakes and ride forward with your blinders on.

Shaping Yourself as CEO

Reshaping your inner CEO to match your outer CEO will be a job in itself. There will be doubt and frustration, tears of sadness and joy, and you may even loose some relationships in the process. And these things are beyond your control. Nothing in life is predictable except that life is unpredictable. Your real estate transactions are unpredictable. It's just best to sit back and make the choice to respond to life in a way that you want to and that meets your vision of the best you. Taking full ownership of your choices is scary because you are vulnerable, exposed, and sometimes alone. The best way to proceed is stop making excuses. Every action has an equal and opposite reaction, so start picking up the phone and make calls, and see how quickly your pipeline is filled with clients waiting to work with you.

Having your team of cheerleaders in place will also provide you with the encouragement needed to proceed. Whether it's a podcast, self-help book, or retreat, have people who are your raving fans in your audience to give you the assurance and the backing required during life's bumps in the road. It continues to be a catalyst for my own personal growth. I love having a coach in my corner. She keeps me grounded in both work and play and reminds me I am not going to die if I fail. It's an investment I choose to make that allows for prosperity and wealth to flow by keeping my channels open for magic. My women's support group continues to fundamentally change my thoughts on the transformative world of business as I know it today. Being part of a greater cause other than myself is the new work world. Additionally, I plan my vacations out in the beginning of the year, one per quarter, so don't stop. Read as many self-help books as you can, continue writing affirmations, and shift your spirituality with daily prayer no matter what the naysayers are saying. Make it a habit to schedule coffee with friends, family, and mentors who will keep filling you up with action steps to move forward.

As a result of reshaping your inner CEO to match your outer CEO, you will keep your real estate business growing on a deliberate path of prosperity and increase your business proposition value, thereby attaining a predictable future of increased success and effectiveness of your real estate sales career. The world will seem easier to navigate, and you will be earning the profits you were born to make. Successful real estate business owners like yourself don't quit. We simply move on to the *NEXT* client to love and serve.

Chapter 12

LADIES COME FIRST— HINDER

*N*ow, you've got your real estate career on the path to earning $100k, but how do you put it all together to transition to a full-time real estate agent and let go of the paycheck? You're going to need a leader and coach to hold you accountable for your daily actions to help position yourself to seek out more business so that you are putting together and delivering a prosperous career.

You know the statistics when it comes to the dropout rate of new agents—87 percent don't continue or renew their license and drop out of real estate as a career because they are unsuccessful at earning the money they thought they would be making after year two. Sad but true—yes, that's Metallica.

And yes, I've seen many talented and capable agents drop out of the business.

After being in real estate for some time, I recall my mentor, let's call her Mom, was on vacation somewhere in the Caribbean. She was always flying off somewhere. She left saying, "You're in charge of the business. Even though we had our own separate real estate businesses, we did share some transactions, and now she was leaving me in charge of her business too. "I won't have any cell service, so make good choices."

Sure, Ma, no problem—my answer to her for everything. My ego was elated.

In that time, I received a call from a very angry seller who was very angry his home had no offers after weeks on the market. He was very angry with the service he was receiving. Did I mention he was very angry?

Confrontation was not my strongest point at the time. I called Mom in a panic and explained to her how angry the seller was, and I informed her she had to call him.

She insisted, "No, I'm on vacation. You can do this."

I kept telling myself, "There's no way I can handle this. He's yelling and screaming. I'm afraid he wants us to release the contract and withdraw the listing." My anxiety was increasing.

Calmly, she stated, "Jennifer, I'm heading in to get a massage. There is no time for me to talk to him as the time zones are different. You can do this." Click!

I called several more times, in a panic, over and over only to leave several messages. It was getting late in the day, she hadn't replied, and I was forced to deal with an uncomfortable situation to the best of my abilities.

Upon her return, she called me and asked about our angry seller and what had happened. I explained to her that dealing with sellers was not my strong point. I wasn't a good negotiator. I didn't have the experience to navigate through this seller, and I couldn't fix the situation. This wasn't my real estate business I was simply a buyer's agent. Then, she explained "If you needed this deal to put food on the table for Jaden to eat, would you have called me?" She was spot on. I was capable of running my own real estate business, and I could deal with all the tribulations it sometimes comes with. The only person capable of earning the $100k in their real estate career was me.

It was my head trash that was getting in the way. My mental garbage was affecting my performance as a real estate sales agent. The head trash was the limiting beliefs, thoughts, and ideas that were preventing me from taking action. It was hindering me from generating the specific result I knew I desired—in this case, earning $100k. My head trash was blocking me from truly becoming the real estate agent I was born to be. I was capable of leaving the band like Chris Cornell and flying solo or maybe even being the lead singer of my own band with my own raving fans.

There will be times in your real estate career that you won't need me to coach you through earning $100k in your real estate business. I won't be able to give you the training to meet your business goals. You have to be the one who wants to do it, and you have to be the one who is comfortable with discomfort. You are the only one capable of making any decision that leads to a salary of $100k in your real estate business.

The process of climbing to the peaks of being a Rock star real estate agent will bring up lots of amazing adventures and glorious results. It will be a mesmerizing experience to the top, and when you get there, you will most likely want to reach further and beyond. This will most likely bring up even more head trash that you will most likely try to avoid. It's OK. It's what's supposed to happen. But this is the way to build your strength and confidence. This is the way you will get raving fans applauding for you to give an encore. This is the way you become a Rock star real estate agent.

ACKNOWLEDGMENTS

A Rock star real estate agent wouldn't be anything without her back-up band. My sincerest thanks to Christina for seeing me through all the knots I've woven myself into, to Mikayla for your flowering surprises of kindness, and to Jackie for your stability during moments of turmoil and disruption, without you and your goal-oriented lists, this book would not have been possible. I am forever thankful. *XOXOXOX*

I am gratefully for working for such a humbling company, EXIT Realty International; motivated by a diligent region, EXIT Realty NY Metro; and supported by an agent centered brokerage, EXIT Realty United. Thank you for bringing out the best in me, and there's still more to come.

A profound applause is due to the many real estate agents I have worked with and completed transactions with over the past years, for you have paved the way for me to come into this business with delight.

Thank you to you and the many real estate agents reading this book and those I have trained over past years in the 7 Saturday's Club. You have enabled me to give my voice and made me believe in myself.

Thank you to Angela Lauria and The Author Incubator's team, as well as to David Hancock and the Morgan James Publishing team for helping me bring this book to print.

And finally, with my dearest heart, thank you to my mentor, Mom, for giving me this gift of reaching for the top and never stopping, for going above and beyond over and over, and showing me there are no limits to what is out there if you just move forward and say, "Next!"

THANK YOU

Thank you so very much for taking the time out of your busy day to read my book, Become a Rock Star Real Estate Agent: 7 Steps to Make $100k. Since you have finished reading this book, I know you are truly on the road to becoming the rock star real estate agent you were born to be.

I am absolutely committed to seeing you succeed and achieve your dreams in a real estate career.

Let's get connected on Instagram #JenniferSeenoTuckerRE and then sign up here https://calendly.com/jenniferseenotucker/conferencecall for a complimentary session with me to jumpstart your plan of action and transform your career in real estate to one filled with moneymaking activities and plenty of closings.

ABOUT THE AUTHOR

 Jennifer Seeno Tucker is an associate broker and vice president of business development of Exit Realty United located in Nassau County, New York. She is the co-creator of the 7 Saturday's Training Program for local real estate agents.

She has helped dozens of real estate agents transition from being a paycheck employee to having a flourishing career as a sole proprietor in real estate. Jennifer has also guided many real estate agents throughout their careers and helped them stay focused in meeting their goals as business owners.

As a former educator with an advanced degree in curriculum design and instruction, Jennifer is committed to utilizing her background to provide real estate agents with the necessary tools for support as they transition to a full-time real estate agent.

In 2017 and 2018, Jennifer was awarded the Silver Award from EXIT Realty International, the seventh-largest real estate brokerage in North America, for her gross closed commissions in the New York Metro region.

As a thank-you to her clients, a portion of Jennifer's commission is donated to a charity of their choice.

Jennifer currently resides in Wantagh, New York, with her daughter and their Chowsky.